All about the
West Highland White Terrier

Arnholme Arrogance of Crinan with his son Swedish Ch Craklewood of Crinan (right)

All about the West Highland White Terrier

BARBARA HANDS

PELHAM BOOKS

First published in Great Britain by
Pelham Books Ltd
27 Wrights Lane
London W8 5TZ
1987

British Library Cataloguing in Publication Data

Hands, Barbara
    All about the West Highland white terrier
    1. West Highland white terriers
    I. Title
    636.7'55   SF429.W4

    ISBN 0-7207-1737-X

Typeset by Sunrise Setting, Torquay, Devon
Printed and bound in Great Britain
by Butler & Tanner Ltd
Frome and London

Contents

The author and publishers are grateful to the following for permission to reproduce photographs: Bushey page 146; Dalton page 24, 104; Thomas Fall page 17; Diane Pearce page 119, Kernick page 85. All the line drawings and the majority of the photographs are by the author.

The breed standard is reproduced by permission of the Kennel Club.

1 History of the Breed

The Beginning of the West Highland White Terrier

The history and development of the West Highland White Terrier is not a long one as up to the end of the nineteenth century it was not known as a separate breed. Any white terriers in a litter were thought to be undesirable and were therefore destroyed. How this situation changed is a legend in the breed history. Whether this legend is true and how much it has been embroidered by time, is a little difficult to tell.

It is probable that the breed was around for many years before it became of interest to breeders at the end of the nineteenth century. There are records dating back to the time of James I (1566 to 1625) where he asked for six little white 'earth dogs' from Argyllshire to be sent as a gift to the King of France. These white 'earth dogs' must surely have been the early ancestors of the breed as we know it today. The first pictorial evidence that we have is a painting by Sir Edward Landseer R.A. of 'Sporting Dogs' and 'Dignity and Impudence'. It was painted in 1839 and shows a hound and a small white terrier in a kennel. The terrier is unquestionably a West Highland, with its small prick ears, dark eyes with piercing expression and jet black nose, it could be nothing else.

The breed started to develop during the later part of the nineteenth century. They were, however, not bred for their show potential but as hard working terriers. They were known for their ability to deal with vermin in the rocky cairns and heather of the Western Highlands of Scotland. Being small they were able to follow small animals such as rabbits, otters and foxes between the boulders which scatter that part of Scotland. At this time the breed seems to have been more varied than at the present time. Dogs weighed from 14 to 18lb (6.4 to 8.1kg) and bitches 12 to 16lb (5.4 to 7.3kg) and measured 8 to 12 inches (20.3 to 30.4cm) at the shoulder.

During the late nineteenth century these white terriers were known by several different names and may have differed in type from one area of

Sir Edwin Landseer.

'Dignity and Impudence' by Sir Edward Landseer. This was on an early post card.

Argyllshire to another. The list of names include the Poltalloch terrier, White Roseneath terrier, White Scottish Cairn and Little Skye. In about 1904 all these names were abandoned and the little white terrier of Scotland became known as the 'West Highland White Terrier'.

Colonel Malcolm of Poltalloch was one of the earliest breeders responsible for the development of the breed in the late nineteenth century. He was known to favour the white dogs in litters of coloured puppies and it is said to be due to an accident he had whilst out hunting. He mistook one of his favourite brown terriers for a hare and shot it. After this tragic accident he limited his breeding stock to 'white' dogs but it took years to develop the strain and breed out the colour.

From photographs and etchings of this period, it is clear that these terriers are strongly related to those of today but with certain obvious differences. The muzzles were much longer and in some dogs it is clear that the noses are not black. They also appear to be much longer cast than the present-day West Highland. A dog that is too short in the loin would be unable to turn in a tight space. As they were used for hunting there was a distinct lack of coat, this being pulled out as they went through the heather.

Colonel Malcolm was by no means the only person to develop the white terrier although his name does seem to have come down to us as the most important one. However, we must also look at the other documented cases.

Dr Flaxman is sometimes credited with the development of the breed. He had a bitch that kept whelping white puppies in her litters. These he kept and after a period of time he produced a strain of white Scottish Terrier. They had good pigmentation and were white or creamy in colour. The strain had hard outer coats and soft undercoats. They were very game

An early mini-post card dated 1904 entitled 'Skye Terriers'. They do look more like West Highlands, even though the one on the right is not holding his ears erect.

and active but pounds lighter than the black Scottish Terrier. Dr Flaxman exhibited his dogs in competition with Colonel Malcolm and they were great rivals in the early show ring.

George Clarke, a gamekeeper at various different Scottish estates, also took a part in the development of the breed by bringing terriers from Mull to Inverary and from there to join the Roseneath terriers at the seat of the Duke of Argyll. No doubt there were many more.

It is a well-known fact that the Scottish Terrier, Cairn and West Highland were all interbred at this time and this did not cease until 1917 when the American Kennel Club stated that 'no Cairn could gain registration if its pedigree carried a West Highland White ancestor within the first three generations'. The Kennel Club in England followed the same line soon afterwards. However it is clear when pedigrees are studied, to what effect one breed affected the other and vice-versa. It is quite interesting that even today Cairns and Scottish Terriers do sometimes have white patches on their chests and a study of the ancestry of some of today's Cairns will throw up a number of West Highlands. For example the Cairn Harviestoun Raider includes a number of West Highlands and

Colonel Malcolm's famous eleven. Note the varying types in this early photograph particularly the difference in leg lengths.

Ch. Morven painted by
F. T. Daws.

Glenmhor Chief, Ch. Glenmhor Pride, Ch. Morven are some of the names that appear.

The West Highland does, from photographs, seem to be a very variable type. For example the photograph of Colonel Malcolm's eleven West Highland White Terriers shows dogs with very varying types of ears, also some are obviously much wider in front than others and there is a great variation in length of leg. Although these things do vary it will be noticed that all have the very characteristic expression and hard coats that we like to have today.

During the early part of the twentieth century the head of the Scottish Terrier became elongated and the West Highland retained the short muzzle and rounder skull.

This was the early beginnings of the breed and from its development we have a dog who was a fearless hunter with a tremendous amount of self-determination. It was small enough and yet strongly built in order to do a day's work in very rugged ground. It had large strong teeth to enable it to kill vermin, a double coat to keep it warm in the inclement weather of the Highlands. One can see from the early development of the breed that although a puppy can be small and very cute, to get the most from your West Highland it must be very firmly handled and not treated as a lap dog or it will rule you and become a menace to everyone. Also as its instinct to chase and kill has been bred for so many years, it is necessary to keep this instinct under control.

At this point it might be interesting to look at the breed standard of the early twentieth century and to compare it with that of the present-day standard to be found in Chapter 2.

No. 1 General appearance: The West Highland White Terrier is a small, game, hardy-looking terrier, possessed with no small amount of self-esteem, with a varminty appearance, strongly built, deep in chest and back ribs, straight back and powerful quarters on muscular legs, and exhibiting in a marked degree a great combination of strength and activity. The coat should be about $2\frac{1}{4}$ inches (5.7cm) long, white in colour, hard, with plenty of soft undercoat with no tendency to wave or curl. The tail should be as straight as possible and carried not too gaily and covered with hard hair but not bushy. The skull should not be too broad, being in proportion to the powerful jaws. The ears should be as small and sharp pointed as possible and carried tightly up and must be absolutely erect. The eyes of moderate size, dark hazel in colour, widely placed with a sharp, bright, intelligent expression. The muzzle should not be too long, powerful and gradually tapering towards the nose. The nose, roof of mouth and pads of feet, distinctly black in colour.

No. 2 Colour: Pure white; any other colour objectionable.

No. 3 Coat: Very important and seldom seen to perfection; must be double-coated. The outer coat consists of hard hair, about 2 inches (5cm) long, and free from any curl. The undercoat which resembles fur, is short, soft and close. Open coats are objectionable.

No. 4 Size: Dogs to weigh from 14 to 18lb (6.4 to 8.1kg) and bitches from 12 to 16lb (5.4 to 7.3kg) and measure from 8 to 12 inches (20.3 to 30.4cm) at the shoulder.

No. 5 Skull: Should not be too narrow, being in proportion to his powerful jaw, not too long, slightly domed, and gradually tapering to the eyes, between which there should be a slight indentation or stop, eyebrows heavy, head and neck thickly coated with hair.

No. 6 Eyes: Widely set apart, medium in size, dark hazel in colour, slightly sunk in the head, sharp and intelligent, which, looking from under the heavy eye-brows, give a piercing look. Full eyes and also light coloured eyes are very objectionable.

No. 7 Muzzle: Should be nearly equal in length to the rest of the skull, powerful and gradually tapering towards the nose, which should be fairly wide. The jaws level and powerful, the teeth square and evenly met, well set and large for the size of the dog. The nose should be distinctly black in colour.

No. 8 Ears: Small, erect, carried tightly up, terminating in a sharp point. The hair on them should be short, smooth (velvety) and they should not be cut. The ears should be free from any fringe at the top. Round, pointed, broad or large ears are very objectionable, also ears too heavily covered with hair.

No. 9 Neck: Muscular and nicely set on sloping shoulders.

No. 10 Chest: Very deep, with breadth in proportion to the size of the dog.

No. 11 Body: Compact, straight back, ribs deep and well arched in the upper half of the ribs, presenting a flattish side appearance, loins broad and strong, hindquarters strong, muscular and wide across the top.

No. 12 Legs and Feet: Both fore and hind legs should be short and muscular. The shoulder blades should be comparatively broad and well sloped backwards. The points of the shoulder blades should be closely knitted into the backbone so that very little movement of them should be noticeable when the dog is walking. The elbow should be close in under the body both when moving and standing, thus causing the foreleg to be well placed in under the shoulder. The forelegs should be straight and thickly covered with short hard hair. The hind legs should be short and sinewy. The thighs very muscular and not too wide apart. The hocks bent and well set in under the body, so as to be fairly close to each other either when standing, walking or trotting. The fore feet are larger than the hind ones, are round, proportionate in size, strong and thickly padded and covered with short hard hair. The hind feet are smaller and thickly padded. The under surface of the pads of the feet and all the nails should be distinctly black in colour. Cow hocks detract from the general appearance. Straight or weak hocks, both kinds, are undesirable and should be guarded against.

No. 13 Tail: 5 or 6 inches (12.7 to 15.2cm) long, covered with hair that is hard with no feather and as straight as possible, carried gaily but not curled over the back. A long tail is objectionable. On no account should tails be docked.

No. 14 Movement: Should be free, straight and easy all round. In front the leg should be freely extended forward by the shoulder. The hind movement should be free, strong and close. The hocks should be freely flexed and drawn close in under the body so that when moving off the foot, the body is thrown or pushed forward with some force. Stiff, stilty movement behind is very objectionable.

Faults

No. 1 Coat: Any silkiness, wave or tendency to curl is a serious blemish as is also an open coat and any black, grey or wheaten hairs.
No. 2 Size: Any specimens under the minimum weight or above the maximum weight are objectionable.
No. 3 Eyes: Full or light coloured.
No. 4 Ears: Round-pointed, drop, semi-erect, also ears too heavily covered with hair.
No. 5 Muzzle: Either under or over shot and defective teeth.

The development of the West Highland for the showring

It is probable that white terriers of some description appeared in the showring in the late nineteenth century although there is no firm evidence that they were West Highlands and certainly no classes were scheduled for the breed under any of its many names. It was in classes of 'Scottish Terriers' where they were shown. In 1899 at the Crystal Palace Show a white Scottish Terrier was amongst the winners, also at that same show Dr Flaxman showed a team of Roseneath Terriers.

The first show to actually classify the West Highland White Terrier was the Annual Show of the Scottish Kennel Club on 26 to 28 October 1904. This was in the same year as the founding of the West Highland White Terrier Club with the Duke of Argyll as its President.

The next show of the S.K.C., in October of 1905, again scheduled classes for the breed and the Championship Certificate was won by Morven who was just $7\frac{1}{2}$ months old. It was in 1907 that Morven became the first Champion of the breed. Ch. Morven's sire was Brogach and his dam was Callaig.

In 1907 two more West Highlands, both owned by the Countess of Aberdeen, gained their titles. They were Ch. Cromar Snowflake, who was by Morven; and Ch. Oronsay. In the same year one hundred and forty-one

West Highlands were registered with the Kennel Club. Also in 1907 Crufts had classes for the breed and the West Highland White Terrier Club of England was formed with the Countess of Aberdeen as President.

In the few years after this the registrations of the breed grew rapidly and many of the names which are now legendary became household names in the breed. Amongst these were Miss Viccars (Childwick), Mr Holland Buckley and his daughter Miss W. Buckley (Scotia), Mrs B. Lucas (Highclere), and Mrs C. Pacey (Wolvey). Mrs Pacey showed a dog called Wolvey MacNab which was born in 1911 but the first of her fifty-eight Champions was made up in 1916. This was Ch. Wolvey Piper born on 24 July 1914 in the same year that she made up Ch. Wolvey Rhoda.

After 1916 all shows were stopped by the First World War and during 1917 and 1918 breeding was prohibited and no dogs born during this period were allowed to be registered except those born under licence. It must have been a soul-destroying time for all dog owners because there was strict food rationing and many dogs had to be destroyed. Some kennels were able to keep a couple of dogs going on anything that they could get and it was these few that made the breeding stock when breeding was allowed again in 1919. During that year one hundred and twenty-six dogs were registered.

A group of West Highlands from the Kennels of Mrs Cameron-Head.

In 1920 shows were restarted and five Champions were made up: Mr C. Viccars' Ch. Charming of Childwick, Mrs B. Lucas's Ch. Highclere Rhalet and Ch. Highclere Romp, Mr J.H. Railton's Ch. White Sylph and Mrs C. Pacey's Ch. Wolvey Skylark.

1904–1920 From 1904 and 1920 there were considerable advances in the breed from its early beginnings and from photographs it is possible to see certain changes taking place in the breed. Although it is only possible to make comments on what is visible in the photographs I think the comments are valid. I do not intend in this early period to mention any dog by name but make more general remarks based on the early photographs I have been able to find.

The earliest West Highlands shown seem to have had little done to them in the way of preparation for the show ring. They looked very much the working terrier which as an extra went to a show. As working terriers they had little hair on the foreface or on the lower legs. The ruff was left as it grew and was in some cases very full. In some cases tails were left untrimmed. In the breed standard of the time it states that the hair on the ears should be short and smooth (velvety) and in early photos all ears appear to be free from long hair. As tails in the same dogs carry heavy coats I think it must be correct to presume that the hair did not grow to any length on the ears. Tails also seemed to have been carried rather lower than we are used to seeing in today's West Highlands. It is very clear from early photographs how closely related to the Cairn these dogs were. They seemed to be rather long in the ribcage or longer in coupling than the present-day West Highland. In many cases front feet turned out. Pigment, although it is rather difficult to see, does seem to have been very good. Although size cannot be commented upon, it is clear from evidence available that the early West Highland was rather longer and lower than today's specimens. As you get nearer to the 1920s there is more evidence of preparation for the show ring. Ruffs seem to be decreasing and tails are tidier. By the 1920s the length to height ratio seems to have shortened. Photographs from the 1923 era show West Highlands which are shorter and more cobby although still with short strong legs, and tails are now held upright without any help from the handler.

1920–1946 Between 1920 and 1939, one hundred and twenty-five Champions were made up, thirty-two being Wolvey, and in 1939 showing ceased until after the Second World War. This time breeding was not banned and food was still available although difficult to get.

During this period there were many famous dogs which did much for

The first champion to be made up after the Second World War was Ch. Freshney Fiametta.

the breed at that time and influenced the breed for the future. Ch. Wolvey Patrician won many Best in Shows and would appear in many extended pedigrees of today's West Highlands. He sired many champions: International Ch. Ray of Rushmoor, Ch. Rodrick of Rushmoor and Ch. Wolvey Wings. Ch. Ray of Rushmoor was the sire of Miss A. Wright's Ch. Calluna Ruairidh who in turn was the sire of Miss M. Turnbull's Ch. Leal Flurry. He was the sire of Ch. Melbourne Mathias who was the grandsire of Furzefield Piper and it was he who was the most prominent sire when breeding and showing restarted after the war in 1946. Unfortunately Piper never became a Champion because of the loss of a tooth.

Studying photographs of these dogs there seems to be little difference between them and some of today's dogs, although again no account can be taken of size. Presumably they were smaller than most of today's show dogs because I have heard many of the older breeders active at that time complaining about the fact that today's dogs are oversize. They seem to typify the section of the breed standard – a small game hardy terrier. It would be very nice to see more of this type, so typical of the breed in the ring today.

1946 to the Present Day Showing began again in 1946 although this was only limited to Breed Clubs. The West Highland White Terrier Club of England held its show in July of that year, the judge being Mrs Winnie Barber. The certificates were won by Timochenko of the Roe owned by The Hon. Torfrida Rollo who gained his title in 1947 and the bitch certificate was won by Macairns Jemima who was made up in 1948. The West Highland White Terrier Club held its show a year later and Miss M. Turnbull was the judge. Her choice for the tickets were Freshney Andy and Betty of Whitehills.

At the next 'of England' show in 1946 the certificates were awarded to Wolvey Prospect and Freshney Fiametta who, by gaining the bitch ticket a year later (1947), became the first post-war British Champion. From the photographs I have seen of her she looks beautiful. 1947 also saw the beginning of the all breed Championship Shows, four Champions being made up in that year.

The standard of the early Champions made up after the Second World War was very high. This may have been due to the fact that the dedicated breeders of the time were only able to run on a few, many being sent to America, so presumably they kept what they considered to be the best. It was from this very limited number of high-quality dogs that breeding commenced after the war. Ch. Melbourne Mathias the last post-war champion and Furzefield Poper who was the sire of nine champions, the most famous son being Ch. Hookwood Mentor who in turn sired eleven champions. One of Mentor's sons was Ch. Barrister of Branston who also sired eleven champions.

In the following years the number of Champions made up grew and are too numerous to mention individually by name. Kennels that had representatives in the list of the 40s, 50s and 60s were: Alpinegay, Backmuir, Birkfell, Branston, Broomlaw, Calluna, Citrus, Cotsmor, Cruben, Crystone, Eriegael, Estcoss, Famecheck, Freshney, Furzefield, Glengyle, Highstile, Hookwood, Incheril, Kendrum, Lasara, Lorrell, Lynwood, Morenish, Petriburg, Pillerton, Quakertown, Rivelin, Shiningcliff, Slitrig, Sollershot, Staplands, Stoneygap, Waideshouse, Whitebriar, Wolvey, Woodpuddle and Wynsolot. This is by no means a complete list of the kennels involved in breeding during these three decades but just shows how popular the breed had become. Many of those who started breeding before the war carried on but many newcomers joined them – some, although sadly not many, are still showing and their knowledge and experience could teach us a great deal today.

From the post-war days until the present time the popularity of the West Highland has increased and registrations at the Kennel Club have also increased annually – the West Highland coming well up in the popularity stakes. The newcomers in the show ring have grown to keep pace with this rise in popularity. Some have joined the ranks for a few years, found the going tough and dropped out, others have come, made up a Champion and disappeared from the show scene. There are very few breeders now showing who were involved in the show scene at the beginning of the 70s. A list of present-day breeders and their affixes will be found at the end of the book.

Dogs from the past which will appear on pedigrees of today

Furzefield Piper: He would, according to Mrs M. Dennis in her book *The West Highland White Terrier*, have become a champion had he not lost a tooth in a kennel fight, for which he was penalised in the ring. This did not prevent him from being the sire of nine champions, the most notable of whom was:

Ch. Hookwood Mentor: He in turn was the sire of a further eleven champions, one of whom was:

Ch. Barrister of Branston: He also sired eleven champions.

Int. Ch. Cruben Dextor: A son of Ch. Hookwood Mentor, who quickly gained his title in this country and was exported to America where he became a prolific sire of champions.

Ch. Calluna the Poacher: He was also successful in the show ring and as a sire will be found on many of today's pedigrees, for he was a popular sire and produced a number of champions in this country and several American champions.

Ch. Alpin of Kendrum: The sire of Ch. Quakertown Quistador and Ch. Dianthus Buttons, who is the only one of the breed to have taken the title of Best in Show at Crufts. This was in 1976. Ch. Alpin's importance as a sire can be seen over many generations of the breed as he himself was born in 1961.

Ch. Pillerton Peterman: Born in 1964 he was a great influence on the breed on both sides of the Atlantic as he went with his breeder to America after being made up in this country. Before leaving England for the U.S.A. he was the sire of eight champions. He can be seen on the pedigree of many of today's successful show dogs.

Ch. Famecheck Hallmark: Sire of ten champions in this country, he also followed many of the other dominant sires to America where he left his mark.

Ch. Sollershot Soloist: Born in 1960, he was by Ch. Bandsman of Branston. Amongst some of Soloist's famous offspring are: Ch. Highstile Prank, Ch. Renlim Rachael, Ch. Lindenhall Drambuie.

The list of champion sires could be almost endless as more champions have been made up in recent years. It is almost impossible to predict which will leave their mark in years to come – only time will tell. Perhaps a glance through the list of winners of the Macconachie Trophy at the end of this book may give some idea of things to come. The winners of this trophy have included:

Ch. Dianthus Buttons: Known to his friends as Bertie, he became a champion in 1974 but it is his greatest win which will make his name live on in the history of the breed. It was in 1976 when Mrs K. Sansom of the Quakertown prefix was judging the breed at Crufts that she found her Best of Breed in Ch. Dianthus Buttons. He went into the Terrier group, on this occasion judged by Mrs Diana Hamilton, a Cairn specialist and all-round

Ch Dianthus Buttons. Best in show: Crufts 1976

judge, who gave him the best in the group. So on to the final where he met and beat the other five group winners, and Mr J. Braddon made him Supreme Best in Show. Bertie was as an adult handled by Geoff Corish, as he was on the occasion of his major win. He was by Ch. Alpin of Kendrum whose breeder was the Hon. T. H. Rollo, out of a bitch called Starcyl Sioux.

Ch. Glenalwynne Sonny Boy: Born in 1972 and owned and bred by Miss J. Herbert. During his long show career which stretched over several years, he was handled by Mr Ernie Sharpe. He became the breed record holder with a total of thirty-three CCs (challenge certificates) with many group wins and Best in Shows to his credit. It is unlikely that this record will be broken as in more recent years it has been the practice of breeders to retire champions in order to bring on a younger dog.

Ch. Cedarfell Merry-n-Bright: Born in early 1970 he quickly became a champion (1971) and had a very successful show career. His success as a sire should also be noted. Glenalwynne Sonny Boy was a son of his but he

The breed's record holder with 33 challenge certificates is Ch. Glenalwynne Sonny Boy. Here he is seen after one of his wins with his handler Mr Ernie Sharpe and owner Miss J Herbert. He is by Ch. Cedarfell Merry and Bright ex Clynebury Silver Kilt.

had many sons and daughters who went on to successful show careers. He was used at stud for many years and died in 1986. He remained much loved by his owner and breeder Mrs M. Coy during his long and active life.

Ch. Domaroy Saracen: A well-known show dog of the late 1970s, he was the winner of the Macconachie Trophy in 1978 and became the top sire in the terrier group in 1982 (Dog World System), gaining most points in that year for progeny gaining CCs and becoming champions.

It is too early to assess the influence of more recent dogs on the breed. Although they can be very popular as stud dogs and extensively used, their value to the breed can only be assessed when it is seen in future stock that they carry the genes to produce good specimens, sticking as far as possible to the breed standard and not merely bowing to the whims of fashion.

Ch. Halfmoon of Olac: She is the bitch CC record holder with fifteen CCs. She was owned and bred by Mr D. Tattersall and became a champion in 1976. Her sire was Eng. and Am. Ch. Olac Moondrift.

So far it is only Champions that have been mentioned as influences on the breed but it is not unheard of for a dog rarely shown to become an influential sire. Newcomers to the breed should consider this point when thinking about future breeding programmes, but this will be looked at at greater length elsewhere in the book. We have an example at the moment in Morenish Just William. He was bred by Miss E. Grieve, his sire being the imported dog English, Swedish and International Ch. Tweed Tartan Caledonier and his dam Ch. Morenish Fanny Macdougal, a great personality. He became the property of Mr G. Corish as a puppy and although shown a few times in the ring was never campaigned to his title due to the fact that his owner was too busy making up other people's dogs. He has sired three champions as well as other CC and championship show winners. The champions being Ch. Crinan Celtic Song and Ch. Clan Crinan and Ch. Drummersdale Ups-a-Daisy. Credit must also be given to the bitch line and in the case of my own two champions, Clan Crinan (D) and Celtic Song (B), their mother was Crinan Celtic Ayre. In her few puppies she had other successful offspring, namely Crinan Charlie Muddle, Valserina of Valucis, J.W. Victor of Valucis at Verndale, Viceroy Valucis J.W.

In recent years the Haweswalton kennel of Mrs S. Hawes has come to the forefront of attention. She has in three successive years won the Macconachie Trophy for Top West Highland White Terrier with three different dogs, namely Houdini, Sportsman and Midshipman. These dogs will make a place for themselves in the history of the breed along with their successors in years to come.

One could go on for pages mentioning successful dogs of the past and present but space is limited. Before drawing a close to this section, mention must be made of the Justrite kennel of Mr and Mrs Ron Armstrong. They have had many successes in the show ring and a constant supply of new champions has been made up by them but I will make special mention of only two. The first, Ch. Jaimont of Whitebriar, was winner of the Terrier group at Crufts in 1984 while Ch. Ballacoar Jinny was Justrite Best in Show at the National Terrier Championship Show in 1986.

It is interesting to look at photographs of dogs of the 70s and 80s and compare them with those of the early twentieth century for certain points are obvious even though it is not wise to judge solely from photographs. The most obvious difference is the development of the coat and the change in presentation from the virtually natural West Highland to the highly trimmed version we have today. A general observation of the ring today will find terriers with much longer legs and narrower fronts, some becoming a little too far removed from the breed standard although to the outsider these terriers look very smart. There is also evidence of longer necks and a shortening of backs although at the same time some dogs can be seen to stand with sloping toplines which can never be considered to be correct.

At a time when there are so many new exhibitors in the breed it would be a good thing for them to sit down and reflect for a while on the most important points of breed type and not get carried away by current fashion.

Ch. Gaywyn Bradey of Branston: The last Branston champion, he was bred by Mrs Dennis and owned by Miss C Owen. Born in 1973 he was by Ch. Alpingay Sonato ex Beautiful Biddy of Branston.

2 Understanding the Breed Standard

The breed standard is the list of points by which all dogs are judged in the show ring. It is drawn up by the Kennel Club. The standard is a guide to breeders and judges to preserve breed characteristics without extremes in shape and temperament destroying the breed. It should be the aim of every breeder to understand the standard thoroughly and to conform as closely to it as possible.

An early breed standard has been quoted already in the book and it is interesting to compare the two.

The Kennel Club is in the process of revising all breed standards so that each standard has uniform headings. This will give a slightly different

Ch. Clan Crinan, top
W.H.W.T. in 1985, also
B.o.B. Crufts 1985.

format to most breed standards. The one for the West Highland White Terrier will be affected to some extent. Although the change is in the character of the layout, very little in the way of change is envisaged in the standard itself. General appearance is to be divided into several different headings: these will be General Appearance, Characteristics and Temperament. Some of the details which appear in the old standard under General Appearance will be moved to make a separate heading of 'Gait' which has not previously had its own section.

General appearance

The general appearance of the West Highland White Terrier is that of a small, game, hardy-looking terrier, possessed of no small amount of self-esteem, with a varminty appearance, strongly built, deep in chest and back ribs, level back and powerful quarters on muscular legs, and exhibiting in a marked degree a great combination of strength and activity. Movement should be free, straight and easy all round. In front, the legs should be freely extended forward by the shoulder. The hind movement should be free, strong and close. The hocks should be freely flexed and drawn close in under the body, so that when moving off the foot the body is pushed forward with some force. Stiff, stilted movement behind is very objectionable.

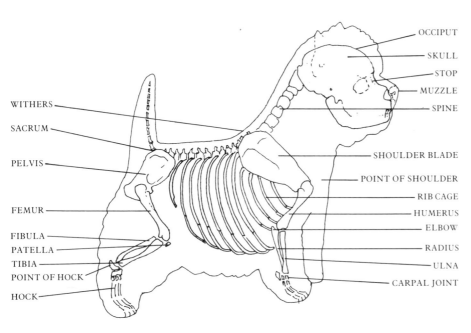

FIG 1 Skeleton of the dog

Head and skull

The skull should be slightly domed and when gripped across the forehead should present a smooth contour. There should only be a very slight tapering from the skull at the level of the ears to the eyes. The distance from the occiput to the eyes should be slightly greater than the length of the foreface. The head should be thickly coated with hair and carried at a right angle or less to the axis of the neck. On no account should the head be carried in the extended position. The foreface should gradually taper from the eye to the muzzle. There should be a distinct stop formed by heavy bone ridges, immediately above and slightly overhanging the eye, and a slight indentation between the eyes. The foreface should not dish or fall away quickly below the eyes where it should be well made up. The jaws should be strong and level. The nose must be black, should be fairly large and forming a smooth contour with the rest of the muzzle. The nose must not project forward giving rise to a snipy appearance.

Eyes

Should be widely set apart, medium in size, as dark as possible in colour. Slightly sunk in head, sharp and intelligent which looking from under the heavy eyebrows imparts a piercing look. Full or light coloured eyes are objectionable.

Ears

Small, erect and carried firming, terminating in a sharp point. The hair on them should be short, smooth (velvety) and they should not be cut. The ears should be free from any fringe at the top. Round pointed, broad, large and thick ears are objectionable, also ears too heavily coated with hair.

Mouth

Should be as broad between the canine teeth as is consistent with the sharp varminty expression demanded. The teeth should be large for the size of the dog, and should articulate in the following manner, the lower canines should lock in front of the upper canines. There should be six teeth between the canines of the upper and lower incisors. The upper incisors should slightly overlap the lower incisors. The inner aspect of the upper incisors being in contact with the outer aspect of the lower incisors. There should be no appreciable space between the incisors when the mouth is closed, ensuring a keen bite; a dead level mouth is not a fault.

Neck

The neck should be sufficiently long to allow the proper set on of the head required, muscular and gradually thickening towards the base allowing the neck to merge into nicely sloping shoulders, thus giving freedom of movement.

Forequarters

The shoulders should be sloped backwards. The shoulder blades should be broad and lie close to the chest wall. The joint formed by the shoulder blade and the upper arm should be placed forward, on account of the obliquity of the shoulder blade, bringing the elbows well in, and allowing the foreleg to move freely, parallel to the axis of the body, like the pendulum of a clock. Forelegs should be short and muscular, straight and thickly covered with short hard hair.

Body

Compact. Level back, loins broad and strong. The chest should be deep and the ribs well arched in the upper half presenting a flattish side appearance. The back ribs should be of considerable depth and the distance from the last rib of the quarters as short as is compatible with free movement of the body.

Hindquarters

Strong, muscular and wide across the top. Legs should be short and muscular and sinewy. The thighs very muscular and not too wide apart. The hocks bent and well set in under the body so as to be fairly close to each other when standing, walking or trotting. Cow hocks detract from the general appearance. Straight or weak hocks – both kinds are undesirable and should be guarded against.

Feet

The forefeet are larger than the hind ones, are round, proportionate in size, strong, thickly padded and covered with short hard hair. The hind feet are small and thickly padded. The under surface of the pads of feet and all nails should be preferably black.

Tail

Five to six inches long, covered with hard hair, no feathers, as straight as possible, carried jauntily, not gay or carried over the back. A long tail is objectionable and on no account should tails be docked.

Coat

Colour pure white, must be double coated. The outer coat consists of hard hair, about two inches long, free from any curl. The undercoat, which resembles fur, is short, soft and close. Open coats are objectionable.

Colour

Pure white.

Size

Size about 11 inches (28cm) at the withers.

Scale of points (as given by the W.H.W.T.C. of England)

	Value
General appearance and size	20
Coat and colour	10
Skull	5
Eyes	5
Muzzle and Teeth	15
Ears	5
Neck	5
Body	10
Legs and Feet	10
Tail	5
Movement	10
Total	100

Clarification of the breed standard

It should be quite evident when looking at the breed standard that the ideal is a small stockily built terrier quite unlike the long-legged terriers. It should be built for work and each of the points of the standard seem to reinforce this. Small and compact with a level back and powerful rear end, it should not resemble the more elegant long-legged terriers in any way. The West Highland is a very active terrier who, as you can see from a glance, thinks a great deal of himself. He is always full of his own importance. He should measure about eleven inches (28cm) at the point of the shoulders and his legs should be short, strong and muscular. He exhibits a combination of strength and activity in a small frame.

He is a friendly terrier and should not display any degree of aggression towards humans. Towards his fellow West Highlands he should be willing to stand up for himself but be friendly. The West Highland was originally worked in a pack and aggression to his fellows should be precluded but this does not mean that he should not be willing to approach a fellow with inquisitiveness, with tail wagging, sounding out whether the other dog is willing to be friendly. He should be willing to show his dominance over another dog by holding his tail up, quivering, ears alert and body 'pulled together', but he should show no aggression or snarling. He should be happy and unafraid with 'no small amount of self-esteem'.

Each of his individual points should reinforce that general character, appearance and temperament.

The skull should be strong and well boned and when going over his head there should be a slight dome between the ears, it should not be flat. The skull itself should be broad and the width at the eyes should be only a little less than its width at the ears.

The length of the skull from between the ears to the eyes should be slightly greater than from the eyes to the nose. The foreface should only taper slightly from the level of the eyes to the nose, giving the muzzle a powerful appearance. The balance of skull and muzzle is very important. If the muzzle is too long and narrow in proportion to the skull the appearance becomes rather snipy. There are other points of importance which give the West Highland its typical expression, without these points

FIG 2 Construction of the head

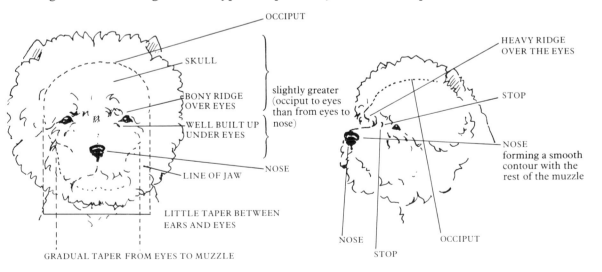

OCCIPUT

SKULL

BONY RIDGE OVER EYES

WELL BUILT UP UNDER EYES

LINE OF JAW

slightly greater (occiput to eyes than from eyes to nose)

NOSE

LITTLE TAPER BETWEEN EARS AND EYES

GRADUAL TAPER FROM EYES TO MUZZLE

HEAVY RIDGE OVER THE EYES

STOP

NOSE forming a smooth contour with the rest of the muzzle

NOSE   OCCIPUT

STOP

the head loses its entire character. Over the eyes there is a heavy bony ridge which makes the eyes look more deeply set giving them a rather piercing expression, combined with this there is a small indentation between the eyes, this is known as the stop. It is not, as many people think, a total indentation of the bone between the eyes but merely a slight dip in the middle of the bridge between the eyes. The arch of bone underneath the eyes should be quite evident when feeling the head. Without this bone formed by the zygomatic arch (cheek bone) the foreface is likely to look and feel rather weak. The bone just mentioned is part of the jaw structure and if this is weak the jaw bone itself is likely to be rather poor. One good point on the foreface leads to others. A strong foreface should be finished off with a fairly large black nose which forms a smooth contour with the rest of the jaw. A small nose which sticks out beyond the rest of the foreface gives rise to a rather snipy appearance. A blunt nose gives the muzzle a shorter look. When assessing the head of a dog in the show ring it is important to remember that head furnishings can give the appearance of something that is not really there. Clever hairdressing can be used to disguise a weak or overlong foreface or a narrow skull. As a judge it is important to assess the proportions of the head without regard to furnishings. The breed standard does call for the head to be thickly coated with hair.

FIG 3 Eye shape and placement

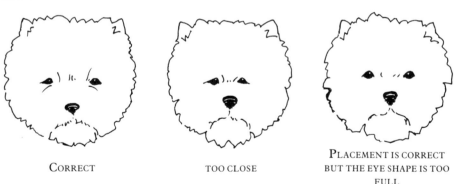

CORRECT   TOO CLOSE   PLACEMENT IS CORRECT BUT THE EYE SHAPE IS TOO FULL

The eye placement and size as well as shape are also extremely important in imparting that typical West Highland expression in addition to the bony ridge over the eyes and the stop between them. Because of their shape and depth of colour they give a very penetrating look which is not gained if they are too round or even light in colour. Although the look should be piercing they should not be small beady eyes. I think the best way of describing the shape is 'almond'. Colour and shape are only part of the picture, placement is also equally important. Even if the eyes are correct in colour and shape if they are placed too close together the expression becomes rather piggy. It is only when they are wide set that the expression is seen to perfection.

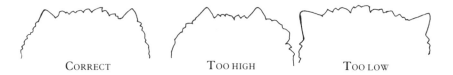

CORRECT   TOO HIGH   TOO LOW

FIG 4 Ear Placement

Whilst still thinking about the perfect head of the West Highland, we must also consider the ears, their size and placement. This is important to complete the picture of an alert, intelligent dog. Unlike the Scottish Terrier which has his ears set well on top of the head, those of the West Highland should be set either side of the head but carried upright. In a mature dog they should be almost but not quite hidden in the dense hair of the head. It is unfair to damn a young dog for the size of the ears because they do tend to grow to their full size before the rest of the dog. It is not until maturity that they can be judged with any accuracy for size. However, shape and placing can be judged earlier. The ears should terminate in a sharp point and the hair on them should be smooth and velvety. Unfortunately ears can sometimes be damaged in puppyhood. A slight scratch on the tip or side of the ear may stop it from growing correctly and hair will be absent from this area of scar tissue. This would make a puppy's show prospects rather dubious. Ear carriage can also add much to the character of the dog. If they are carried too close on top of the head, there seems to be a continual look of surprise about his expression. Too low and he can impart a rather mulish expression. West Highlands, being such characters, can express a lot of their feelings by the way they use their ears and it can be very exasperating in the show ring if he folds his ears back whilst looking up at you lovingly! It is important to try and attract the dog's attention in some way so that the ears are held correctly for the judge to assess.

Finally we must look at the jaw and teeth of the West Highland. The present standard goes into great detail about how the teeth should articulate. In fact all that is being described in detail is the perfect, regular scissor bite. It is probably very difficult for a beginner to understand this section and is more easily seen in drawing and photographic illustrations. It is nice to see a good bite with teeth set straight in the gum and a rare delight to see a set of large beautifully spaced teeth broad between the canines. There should be six teeth between the canine teeth of the upper and lower jaw, it is not uncommon to find less than the required number. Although in this country the number of teeth in the dog's mouth, apart

FIG 5 Overshot bite
and FIG 6 Undershot
bite

from canines and incisors, is not considered important, some countries insist on either a full complement of forty-two teeth or something very close to that. So for a dog destined for the continental show ring it is important to check the teeth after the adult set is through. There should be twelve incisors, which are the front teeth, six on each jaw. Then the four canines, one at each end of the incisors. Behind the canine teeth are the

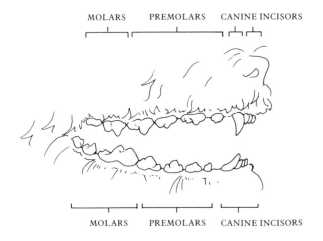

FIG 6a A full mouth of 42 teeth. The diagram shows half the mouth.

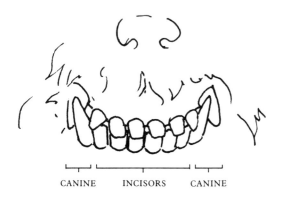

FIG 7 A regular scissor bite.

pre-molars, fourteen in all, four being on each side of the lower jaw and three on each side of the upper one. Finally come the twelve molars, three on each side of each jaw.

As well as missing and twisted teeth which do not look very attractive, faults can be caused by the way the jaw closes. An undershot mouth is when the teeth of the lower jaw close in front of those in the upper jaw. Sometimes there is a gap between the teeth in addition to the incorrect bite. The overshot mouth is when the teeth in the upper jaw close in the correct manner but there is a gap behind the upper teeth and in front of the lower. This type of bite is quite often seen in young puppies changing to their adult teeth. The upper jaw sometimes grows more quickly than the lower one, but by the time the puppy has finished teething this condition usually rights itself. An undershot mouth in a young puppy is extremely unlikely to correct itself on the completion of teething.

FIG 8 Neck sets

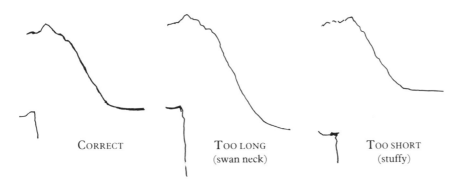

CORRECT

TOO LONG
(swan neck)

TOO SHORT
(stuffy)

The neck should not be long and swan-like for although this may attract attention in the show ring it detracts from the character and breed type. It should be of sufficient length to allow the head to be carried correctly and it should be muscular. It should be broad enough at its base to allow for the correct shoulder placement. A long thin neck usually means that the shoulders are placed in an upright position. The shoulders of the dog have to be assessed from both the side and the front. From the side the joint formed by the upper arm and the shoulder blade should be placed well forward and the shoulder blade itself should be broad and flat. From the front of the dog the forelegs should be straight, short and muscular and the gap between them should be enough to take about the width of the hand. This distance is governed by the rib cage. Legs that are too close together

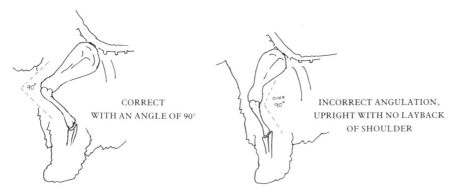

CORRECT
WITH AN ANGLE OF 90°

INCORRECT ANGULATION,
UPRIGHT WITH NO LAYBACK
OF SHOULDER

FIG 9 Shoulders

are likely to be so because the ribs are not well enough arched in their upper half. Barrel ribs would be likely to set the front legs too wide apart causing the dog to roll whilst on the move. The elbows should be well tucked in to the sides of the rib cage allowing the legs to move freely when in motion. The movement made by the front legs when the dog is on the move should resemble the movement of the pendulum of a clock, swinging easily in a straight line from the shoulder.

The body of the West Highland should be compact and muscular. A level back is a necessity and it is important, when standing your dog for the judge's inspection, that he keeps his level top line. Too often one finds the hind legs drawn so far out behind the dog that the top line slopes from the shoulder to the tail. The rib cage is most important in achieving the correct shape called for in the standard. It should arch well in the upper half giving plenty of room for heart and lungs after the arch the sides of the dog should be flat, as without the arch the dog would be rather narrow when viewed from the front. The depth of the back ribs should be considerable giving the body a very cobby appearance. One often sees the comment in the reports of the breed from shows that a particular specimen has a short back. In fact the breed standard does not mention this point. What is called for is that the distance from the last rib to the quarters be as short as possible whilst still allowing the dog to move his hind legs freely. This is known as being 'short coupled'. It is probable that a bitch will be slightly longer in coupling than a dog as more room is required for her to carry a litter of puppies. The short coupling combined with the correct lay-back

FIG 10 (LEFT) Correct front FIG 11 Correct rear FIG 12 Diagram showing barrel which leads to a wide front FIG 13 Diagram showing a dog with a long coupling

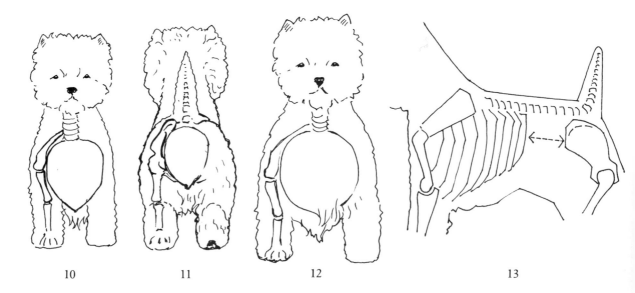

10   11   12   13

of the shoulders will of course lead to a shorter back, but it is important for the novice to realise what makes this happen. The hindquarters should be broad and muscular, in fact taking a bird's-eye view of the West Highland it should be somewhat wedge-shaped and viewed from behind it should be impossible to see beyond the rear to the shoulders. If the shoulders can be seen from the rear it could be that the shoulders are rather heavy but it is more likely that the hindquarters are too narrow. This fault is most seen with the terriers that are also too long in the leg, giving them the shape foreign to the breed. The hind legs should also be strong and muscular, the second thigh being of importance. The tops of the thighs should really be considerable, lack of the second thigh which is formed by the Satorius, gracilis and adductor muscles is likely to lead to rather poor movement. Dogs with the correct strong driving movement can be found to have the correct muscle formation. The lower parts of the hind legs should be well placed under the body when viewed from the rear, they should not project sideways outside the line of the upper parts of the legs. Nor should they be too close together. The hocks themselves should be parallel to each other, and not cow-hocked or bow-legged. The angle of the pelvis and femur leads to a correct stifle angulation and gives the rear a nicely rounded appearance when viewed from the side. It should not be possible to drop a line directly from tail to ground without encountering the thigh and hock.

   The forefeet are larger than the hind ones but all should be round and thickly padded. The pads and all nails should be black if possible. All too often good feet can be spoilt by the lack of a regular pedicure. Short toe nails allow the dog to grip and encourage the tight foot. If the nails are allowed to grow long the foot itself starts to spread.

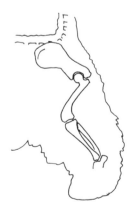

CORRECT ANGLE OF PELVIS

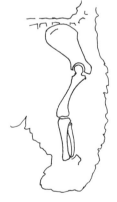

AN UPRIGHT PELVIS LEADS
TO A LOWSET AND
STRAIGHT STIFLE

FIG 14 Rear angulation

FIG 15 Tail sets

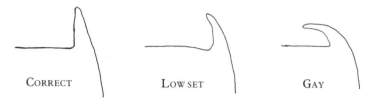

CORRECT   LOW SET   GAY

FIG 16 Outline showing
several undesirable points,
most unlikely to be found
in one dog

(a) Sloping top-line
(b) Upright shoulder
(c) Straight stifle

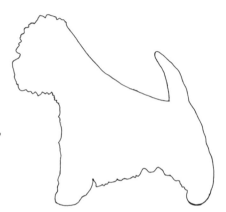

The tail of the West Highland is not docked and its natural length should be about five to six inches (13 to 15.5 cm). It should really balance with the rest of the dog probably being level with the crown of the head. A tail which is overlong spoils the balance of the dog. The tail should be held as straight as possible and carried jauntily. When moving, the tail finishes off the lively movement seen in the West Highland. It would be rather unnatural to see the tail held as rigid as a poker whilst the dog was on the move. It should still however be held straight and not held in a curve over the dog's back, nor should it be carried out behind the dog in the manner of the Cairn Terrier.

The movement of the West Highland should be very free. The picture of a dog moving correctly always brings to mind a Scotsman in a kilt trotting away into the distance. The front legs should be extended forward by the shoulder. The hind legs should push the body forward with some force, extending well backward. The hocks, after pushing the body forward, should be drawn well under the body ready to take the next step. The strides taken by each step are quite considerable for the size of the dog, so he should cover a lot of ground with each stride. Proper movement requires the correct structure, upright shoulder will prevent the correct reach in front and straight hocks do not give enough angulation to allow the driving action behind. An incorrect rear structure would give a rather stiff, stilted and bouncy movement which should be considered as a fault.

The coat is most important to the overall appearance of the West Highland but is seldom seen to perfection. The coat should be double and white. The undercoat is short and resembles fur, it should be dense. It is this coat that keeps the dog cool in summer and warm in winter for it acts rather like a string vest, trapping the air to maintain an even temperature.

The outer coat is longer than the undercoat being about 2 inches (5.1cm) long on the body. It should be absolutely straight and very harsh when compared with the under coat. The colour of the coat is rather a silvery-white, a softer coated dog may look whiter in the show ring next to a dog with the correct type of coat which can look a little grey by comparison. It is this coat which protects the dog from the elements and makes his jacket virtually water-proof.

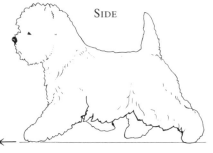

SIDE

FIG 17 Movement

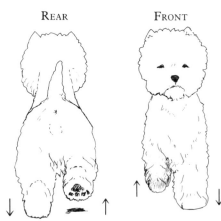

REAR   FRONT

The show dog has a coat of varying length. The shoulder coat is very short and the undercoat is largely groomed out in order to allow the coat to lie flat. The hair is gradually left longer down the neck and onto the body where it should be two inches long. Many show dogs do not have the desired length of coat, the coat on the back in some cases resembling that on a Wire Fox Terrier. Sometimes a yellow dorsal strip appears, unfortunately some dogs have this fault permanently but it is more usually seen in dogs that are between coats. An examination of the individual hair usually shows the colour only at the tip of the hair and if it is left to grow a little the colour seems to disappear.

The West Highland is a small terrier and should measure approximately eleven inches (28cm) at the shoulder. How much over or under this standard the judge is willing to accept seems to be very variable. Although the male should be a little bigger than the female it is not necessary to measure an inch or two over the standard to look masculine; it is by his whole bearing and structure that the dog should look all male.

The breed standard sets out very precisely what we as breeders should aim for in the perfect specimen and it is what every judge should have in mind when assessing a West Highland. How each breeder and judge interprets this standard does however lead to some variations.

It should also be remembered that no dog however good is perfect but it is perfection we should try to aim for when the future of the breed is in our hands.

3 Choosing a Puppy

Before choosing your puppy it is necessary to decide what you want a puppy for: some reasons may be totally selfish and a puppy may not really be suitable for you. It would never be correct to have a puppy if, for instance, you were out at work all day or were on a constant whirl of social engagements, as it must be remembered that they will take up a great deal of your time in their early months and will continue to require much attention all their lives. The more work and attention you give to a young puppy, the more love and devotion they will give to you.

Having decided that you want a puppy as a companion to take an important role in the household, you must then think about what, if anything, else you would like him to be able to do – show or obedience because each of these roles requires different qualities, many of them can overlap but a good companion may not necessarily be a good show dog.

General points to look for when choosing a puppy

A puppy's future health and wellbeing start long before his birth when the owner of the bitch decides to have her mated. Her health and mental attitude should be taken into account when looking at a litter of puppies. From that point of view it would be essential to go where it is possible to see the mother and the way she is treated, fed and housed. Remember that not all West Highlands will be house pets living with the family; but even living in kennels she should have a warm dry bed and draught-free housing. The bitch in whelp or with puppies should not have to compete with her fellows for food or a bed. The best-run kennels have separate accommodation for the bitch who is about to have puppies and for nursing them. To rear the puppies as well as she is able she needs peace of mind and freedom from the competition of her kennel mates.

A good breeder realises that this is so important to the quality of the ensuing litter and it would be wise for the prospective pet owner to search out such a breeder and wait if necessary to get a quality puppy from the breeder of their choice. I think the number one point to remember is that

A quality puppy at eight weeks old. She is now at the age when you should start to remove puppy fluff.

the choice of your puppy is of prime importance, do not go to a particular establishment because you can 'get a puppy tomorrow'.

The growth in popularity of the 'Westie' has made it all too easy for you to acquire a specimen of the breed and several sources of supply are now open to you. Unfortunately, due to the popularity of the breed at the moment it is all too easy to make a mistake which you may regret for years. Recently media attention has been drawn to so-called 'puppy farms' where gain is the object of the owners and not the health and wellbeing of their stock. A prospective buyer must beware of falling into the trap of purchasing from this type of establishment or puppies from a similar source. It is wise to ignore advertisements in the press where several breeds are mentioned, for the source of supply to these establishments is invariably a puppy farm. No breeder caring about his stock will sell litters wholesale for some other source to sell on. It would be unthinkable to sell a litter of puppies to someone at six weeks old only to have them transported around the country to distant destinations. They may appear in a local pet shop window and be very tempting but never buy a dog on impulse. We have a thriving Westie Rescue Scheme that is kept very busy, very few of these dogs are from recognised breeders but from unknown names usually in the more rural parts of Wales and Scotland.

You may now be saying to yourself 'but how can I find a reputable source of supply?' There are several means open to you where you will find help. You will need patience and perseverance to follow these to a satisfactory conclusion but in the end you will find it very worthwhile. Your first enquiries should be to the Kennel Club in London, their address and telephone number can be found at the end of the book. They may do two separate things. Either they will refer you to the breed club secretaries or give you the name of someone in your area whose name and address is known to them because their dog has appeared in the *Kennel Club Stud Book*. The next step is to contact one of these sources. It is very unlikely that the secretaries or stud dog owners will have puppies available themselves but they will be able to help further by passing you down the line and giving you more information in passing. The stud dog owners will be able to give you the names and addresses of people who have brought bitches to be mated to their stud dogs. These bitches are not necessarily show bitches, in fact they are most likely to be the family pet bitch, but in this case the puppies are a single litter that has been well reared in the house. You may be given the name of someone else to contact, you may be thoroughly cross-examined to find out if you are suitable to pass on to someone with puppies but I consider this to be one of the signs of a caring breeder. The secretaries will be able to pass you on to someone in your area who is a member of one of the breed clubs.

Puppies at 3 weeks of age, showing varying degrees of pigment on the noses; all were eventually black.

It is probable that you will have to wait some time or travel some distance to purchase a suitable puppy but this should not be considered a disadvantage.

Puppies should not be purchased for a particular date (e.g. 25 December) but when a puppy suitable to your requirements is available to you. This may indeed necessitate a delay of several weeks or even months but the wait will usually be well worthwhile and is a very useful time for preparing to adopt the new member of the family.

Having found a reliable source for your new puppy, there are certain questions that you will probably be asked and it is a good idea to have thought about them beforehand.

Do you want a companion or a show dog?

A breeder who is breeding a litter to try and improve his strain will rear the whole litter to the highest possible standards, therefore there will be no difference in the rearing of the 'best' and the 'worst' puppy in the litter. With the knowledge of his strain in mind he will usually have a very good idea about how the puppies are developing. His knowledge of the breed standard and previous litters will give him an excellent idea about which puppies are show prospect and which should be considered as a companion. It is not, however, possible at the age of buying a puppy at say eight weeks, to say the chosen puppy is a 'show puppy', because many things can and do go wrong in the time between two and six months. All puppies should be sold as companions with some considered to have show potential and others as pure companions. In this age of litigation and consumer protection it would be very unwise for any breeder to guarantee a very young puppy as to its future in any way, either show quality or in health. We all hope that a small puppy sold at a young age will be a superb example of its breed and lead a long and healthy life but as a purchaser this is one of the risks that must be taken and if you consider it sensible, suitable insurance can be taken out as a protection for the future. A wise breeder may even sell the puppy with some sort of initial insurance to cover the puppy for the first few weeks in its new home and advise the new owner to continue the insurance.

Before going to see a litter of puppies, make yourself familiar with the breed standard and try to understand as much as you can about it. This is a good idea as it will give you a little understanding about what you are looking at. Puppies at four or five weeks old have started to develop a character of their own and it is important to try and pick the character of the puppy that would best fit in to that of the prospective new home.

If you are looking solely for a companion, the sex of the puppy matters very little. I have often had a prospective owner say to me that they have been told that a bitch is less likely to wander. If responsible pet ownership is encouraged neither sex should be allowed to wander as they should be kept under control at all times. As for being more faithful, that depends very largely on a developing bond between dog and owner and is very little to do with the sex of the animal. In many ways a dog is less trouble for the companion as you do not have to worry about the breeding cycle of the female. This can cause problems not for you as the responsible pet owner but from the other irresponsible members of the public who allow their dogs to wander. Remember it is not the dog who is the nuisance but the owner who fails to teach the dog anything and exercises no control over it. There are also some misconceptions about the characters of dogs and bitches. It is often thought that bitches have a very sweet lovable nature and are easier to train. On the contrary some bitches can be real 'tom-boys' and it is just as likely that you can have an affectionate dog. Choose the puppy for its character and not its sex.

If you have an outgoing personality and there are children in the family then a puppy with this type of character is the best type for you. An older quieter person who has a more gentle personality should try to pick a similar temperament to themselves as they would find a boisterous puppy too much for them to handle. The shy nervous puppy who cowers at the back of the pen is not always a wise choice as it would need to be handled with great care and understanding to allow for the development of a well-balanced puppy. Wrong handling of this type of puppy could easily turn to aggression.

By the time the litter has reached six weeks it is possible to assess the type of coat the puppy has. A good-coated puppy would at this age look rather smooth in coat and quite plain. On the other hand the soft-coated puppy would look a bundle of fluff and very appealing but it is a very difficult coat to manage as the coat never becomes any better. In adulthood the only option you would have with this coat is to cut or scissor it. There is an in-between type of coat which at this age looks slightly fluffy, it is rather wispy and thin. After hand stripping it usually becomes quite hard and perfectly acceptable as a show coat. This type of coat would develop more head and leg hair at an earlier age. The hard-coated puppy, although it does not look as appealing at the time is the correct one and provided that it has a double coat would be the best to choose for a show prospect. Some idea of coat type can be seen by looking at the dam of the puppies although by the time you see her she will probably look rather thin and the quality of her coat could well have deteriorated due to loss of condition while feeding the puppies. The main aim for the pet owner at this stage is to find a puppy from an overall sound and healthy litter, clean and well nourished, relaxed and happy. It does not matter at this age whether ears are up or down and the teeth are only just coming through so it is a little too early to look at them in too much detail.

The breeder of a litter will spend hours watching and assessing the puppies and it is from them that you the prospective owner can gain a lot of knowledge and help in finding which puppy would be best for you.

FIG 18 Puppy shape at about 8 weeks old showing (*Left*) large feet which appear to turn out. One ear up, the other down and (*Right*) level topline, good tail set and bend of stifle.

The puppy at eight weeks

It is never possible to breed the perfect Westie. When being very critical some fault or imperfection can always be found. It is very difficult to choose a puppy at eight weeks old that, when mature, will be a certain champion. There are, however, points that can be noted which may be useful when trying to choose your puppy from a litter. I have mentioned in the previous section the more obvious points of general condition and coat type but now let us look in greater detail at some of the finer points that could be noted.

When puppies are born their noses and pads are usually pink and over a period of time will turn black. The time can vary from hours to weeks and the pigment can change in two ways. In the first the whole nose and pads will gradually change from pink through grey to black. Sometimes all the pads will be black but sometimes they will be patchy. This also applies to the nails. It would be preferable if they were all black but this is seldom seen to perfection. They can be striped whitish and black or even pink but the nearer to black the better. The other way in which the nose changes pigment is in spots. Small black spots appear on the nose, these gradually grow and as time passes the black spots grow larger and the amount of pink decreases. In this case the pigment takes longer to change and in looking at an eight-week-old puppy it would be possible to see some pink still remaining. I have known a prospective purchaser reject an otherwise excellent puppy because a small pink spot was still visible on the nose. Through personal experience I have found that pigment coming in this way is less likely to fade. My first champion had a pink spot which finally disappeared at the age of five months and at thirteen years of age her nose is still jet black. This will vary from one line to another but a breeder would be able to advise you on what is usual in their particular strain.

At this age a West Highland is rather square and boxy and should feel relatively heavy when picked up, this being due to good feeding and rearing and the presence of plenty of bone. A light shelly puppy is unlikely to be able to make up for the poor start in life and it is probable that it will grow up to be a poor specimen of the breed. Ears at this age can be carried erect or folded forward over the face, either is correct. Sometimes one will be up and one down leading to a rather comical expression. They can vary a lot in size as ears tend to grow before the rest of the body. Irrespective of size or whether they are up or down it is the set of the ears which is important. When the puppy's attention is gained, the ears should form almost an equilateral triangle with the eyes and the nose. If they are too far down the sides of the head this gives a rather mulish expression. Placed too high on the head and there is a look of a little girl with a ribbon tied in a bow on top of her head. The correct 'Westie' expression is gained partly by the set of the ears.

The skull itself should be broad, as should the muzzle giving plenty of room for the puppy teeth which at this point are like little needles. You will find that puppy teeth at this stage are very well spaced. If they are crowded together, the adult teeth will almost certainly be the same. If you are looking for a puppy with show potential, count the incisors, both top and bottom. There should be six in each jaw. It would be a risk to take a puppy with the incorrect number of teeth because the adult set is usually the same. However, for a pet this does not matter at all because it will have little effect on the puppy's ability to eat.

The eyes of a puppy at this age should be very bright and clear. They should be very dark in colour, the bluish tint that they have when the eyes first open should, at this stage, have completely disappeared. If they appear to be light in colour at this age and the pupil is easily detectable from the surrounding colour it is certain that they will have light coloured

Correct ear placement and eye shape in a young puppy.

The same head shape but with eyes too round and ears too high set.

The same head shape but with eyes too close set and ears too low.

FIG 19 Puppy heads

eyes as an adult. As well as the colour of the eyes their shape and placing are of importance. Eyes should have a rather keen piercing expression and they should not be too close together. Round or full eyes do not give that typical expression of the breed.

The body at about this age is about the same height as its length although this is something which can vary from one line to another. Excessive length to height will usually be the same in adulthood. To finish the body the tail should be held at almost right angles to the body and carried as straight as possible. Some puppies who get rather excited are inclined to carry their tails rather gaily. Like the ears, the tail is the part of the body that grows ahead of the rest but it should be thick at the root and taper to a point and not docked. The tail should be straight without any kinks and these are easy to detect in a youngster at this stage.

The front legs of the puppy should be quite stocky and when viewed from the front should appear straight. Some puppies have huge feet which can appear to make the legs turn out. It is necessary to feel down the front legs to assess them better, as leg hair can also detract from the straight appearance at this stage. The hind legs of a puppy should show a good bend of stifle and views from the side should show a definite bend of the legs giving that distinct bottom which is so nice to see in a West Highland puppy. A puppy that is straight in stifle will stand with its legs tucked well under the body and an imagined line dropped from tail to floor would be clear of the rest of the puppy.

The temperament of the puppy can also be assessed. A puppy that has a bold, full-of-the-joys-of-spring attitude to life will be harder to train but provided the conformation is correct he should be a good showman. A puppy that is a little shy may be like that because of the other very dominant puppies in the litter and may be fine when removed from them but in any case he could certainly become a super companion as he is allowed to develop his own character away from more dominant puppies.

If you are choosing a dog puppy for its show potential as opposed to a bitch, you should check that it is 'entire'. This means that both testicles should be properly descended in the scrotum. This should be easy to check at three months of age and whilst it is not impossible for them to descend after three months of age, it becomes more chancy.

Preparation at home

So now you have chosen your puppy and depending on when the breeder lets you see the litter they may be between six and eight weeks old. Before you take the puppy home there are certain preparations you should make. Presumably, if you have chosen to have a dog you will have some sort of garden or enclosure at the rear of your property where a dog can be safely contained and this should be considered first. You may look at the fencing and say that it is in good condition but take a very close look at the bottom where the fence or hedge meets the earth. The 'Westie' being a terrier would take only a few scrapes with his strong paws to make that tiny gap big enough to squeeze through. The first thing a small puppy will want to do is to make a close inspection of his new territory and on finding a small gap will want to see where it goes to. If you have a hedge it is a wise precaution to dig a small trench under it and insert a length of fine chicken wire into this. If it is 24 inches (.6m) high the base can be covered again by soil or something more permanent and the rest of the wire kept in place by stakes held at regular intervals. The hedge will soon grow through the fine mesh and obscure it from view. Weather boarding is very secure but again check the bottom especially if there is any change in level of the ground. It is amazing into what tight corners a 'Westie' puppy can crawl. They are inquisitive by nature and you as a responsible dog owner must be aware that his desire to be into everything must be watched carefully. This includes a garden pond. Care must be taken to cover it safely as it would be all too easy for a puppy to fall in and drown.

Now to the house itself. Lie down on the floor and consider it from the point of view of a mischievous puppy. He would not be able to tell the difference between that piece of rope you were going to let him play with and the piece of electric cable snaking invitingly across the floor and an open invitation to sink his teeth into. If at all possible all cables should be well out of reach of young puppies or you should be on constant guard when the puppy is playing loose near the cables. Plants at ground level are a definite temptation to puppies and some can cause severely upset tummies, also it may be as well to raise that valuable 'Ming' vase just a little higher off the floor!

Sleeping quarters

Before the puppy arrives decide where he is going to sleep in the house and in what. Until he is house-trained it is probably a good thing to make a small area in the kitchen in which the puppy can be contained at night and which can be removed during the day. It can also be used to pen the puppy in safely if you are leaving the house for a short while. It is possible to buy panels of the type used for garden incinerators which are ideal for this purpose, also plastic-coated ridged wire panels are readily available. The panelling should be about 18 to 24 inches (46 to 61cm) high, as by this time 'Westies' can climb over anything much less than this. It is possible to purchase many types of dog beds ranging from the 'four-poster' to the more humble bean-bag, but for a puppy the simpler the better. It is unwise to purchase a permanent bed straight away because a bed should fit the size of the dog. A small puppy left by himself in a large dog basket would feel very insecure. My suggestion is a cardboard box of a suitable size for the puppy. This can be thrown away when it becomes too small or soiled in any way. The box should be big enough for the puppy to stretch out full length and also to take a blanket. Having said this, a 'Westie' always seems to jam itself across the smallest space. Cut out virtually the whole of one long side of the box leaving several inches at either side of the opening and at the bottom for added strength. As the puppy grows exchange the small box for one a size bigger. This can be continued until the puppy has reached about the age of six months. He will also respect his new bed a little more by this age and with luck will have got over the chewing stage. Be careful when choosing the cardboard box that it has not been used to pack any harmful substances as this could leave behind small amounts of the substance which would make the puppy sick.

When the puppy is old enough for his permanent bed there are many different types to choose from. When considering which one to choose, several different points should be taken into account; I think the most important is hygiene. The best as far as this is concerned is an oval plastic bed. These are usually brown in colour with a slightly rough surface. This can be thoroughly scrubbed and disinfected at intervals and so discourage undesirable visitors and infections. The blankets you choose to place in the bed should also be easily washable and can be of many types. Cotton and flannelette can be used for summer bedding and one of the many types of fur blanket specially manufactured for pet bed use would be better for colder weather.

Other types of bed available on the market which are suitable are woven baskets which are made in various sizes. A new development is the bean-bag. These are also available in different sizes and are made with detachable covers which can be made to suit your own furnishing scheme. Both the bag and cover can be washed when necessary. Other types of bed are made in foam plastic covered in fur and fabric but these are rather more difficult to wash.

You should now be prepared for the day when your puppy is ready to join you in his new home.

Collecting the puppy

Do not go by yourself to collect the puppy as it can be very difficult to concentrate on driving as well as comforting and talking to the new baby. Take with you a high-sided cardboard box with a piece of old blanket in the bottom. This will allow the puppy to curl up in the bottom and feel quite safe. A young puppy travelling in a car for the first time could well be travel sick so unless your knee is well covered with a towel and you are prepared for this it is better that the puppy is placed in the box. When going to collect your puppy it is better to go early in the day and allow plenty of time for asking questions and talking to the breeder. They will probably want to check with you that you have everything ready for the new puppy. Do not feel offended if you are asked unexpected questions which you think are personal, they are for the good of the puppy and the peace of mind of the breeder.

There are several things which you should get from the breeder after accepting the puppy. Perhaps the most important as far as the well being of the puppy is concerned is a diet sheet. This should give you very clear instructions of when and what to feed the puppy. Read it over carefully and make sure that you understand it. The diet should give quantities as well as type of food to be given at each meal. When you go home stick as closely to this diet as possible as any change that you make may upset the digestive system of the puppy. After a time, when the puppy has settled in, you can start to vary the diet. As well as food you should also make a note of any additive that is being given to the puppy so that you can continue with the same feeding programme. A caring breeder may even give you small samples of the food the puppy has been having, so reassuring herself that the puppy will continue on the correct diet until you are able to purchase some of a similar type. If you are at all concerned that you may not be able to get the particular type of food that is on the diet sheet and you are not offered any by the breeder, offer to buy a small amount from her until you are able to make a gradual change of diet.

You should also be given a clearly written pedigree of your puppy. This should be signed by the breeder and is your record of the puppy's breeding. An experienced breeder takes great care in writing this out because a mistake in spelling or in dogs mentioned could cause problems for you in the event of your wanting to reproduce the pedigree. If you are buying a puppy with any terms and conditions attached to the sale you should also get a receipt stating the terms so that there can be no misunderstanding from either party. A breeder may endorse a pedigree with such terms as, 'not for breeding' or 'not for competition' or 'sold as companion or pet only' so that it is clear that no attempt is being made to sell you an animal of show quality. If this is the case you should be told if there is any obvious fault, bearing in mind the breed standard, and if you feel that this is unacceptable to you you should not buy the puppy. There is also another document that is important and that is the Kennel Club Registration Certificate. There are two types:

1. Registration of the puppy only, no name given. In this case you can name the puppy with a name of your choice at the Kennel Club, or you may if you wish do nothing at all. If there is any chance that the puppy will be shown or bred from you should register it as soon as possible because registration can take several weeks.

2. Registration of the puppy by the breeder. In this case the breeder will choose a name for the puppy and this will include the affix which is the 'family' name of that breeder, registered at the Kennel Club. You may not register your puppy with this name as it has protection by the Kennel Club and may be used by the breeder only. In the case of this type of registration the reverse side of the registration form should be filled in and signed by the breeder so that you can transfer the puppy into your name at the Kennel Club.

The registrations may not be available at this time as it may take several weeks to get them through from the Kennel Club and most breeders do not apply for them until the puppies are several weeks old. It is a good idea to make sure that the registration process is in progress and that you will get the papers as soon as they are available.

As the paperwork is now complete take a little time to talk to the breeder and ask any questions that may be bothering you. If dog ownership is new to you and you live near the breeder there are other things that may be useful such as the name and address of the local vet and the best pet shop to patronize.

You are now responsible for your new acquisition and it is time to take over from the breeder and start off a new life for the puppy.

4 Looking after your new Puppy

Settling in

Having received all the information and help that you can get from the breeder it is time to leave for home. This will probably be rather a disturbing time for the new puppy and everything possible should be done to make him or her feel as secure as possible. Place the puppy in the cardboard box you have brought with you, making him as comfortable as possible on a blanket at the bottom. If you are collecting the puppy in winter and the weather is very cold, a hot water bottle wrapped up in an old towel or woolly would possibly add to his comfort. If you had to collect the puppy on your own, place the box on the floor of the car in front of the passenger seat, making absolutely sure that he cannot climb out and interfere with your feet whilst driving. If you have been able to take a driver with you, it is better to sit on the back seat with the puppy next to you. The driver should be asked to drive as carefully as possible, especially at roundabouts so as not to swing the puppy around too much.

On arriving home, it would be all too easy to invite everyone in to see the new arrival, but resist this temptation. Take the puppy into his own sleeping quarters and show him his new bed. Offer a small drink of warm milk with perhaps the addition of a little glucose. If the puppy then wants to sleep, leave him alone and allow him to do so. If you have small children keep them well away so that he can rest without any disturbance.

Some puppies will not be in the least bothered by the journey but it is wise to introduce them to their sleeping quarters first. It should be made a very strict rule in the household that at any time should the puppy retire to his bed he should be left alone and not woken up 'to be played with'. He will then know that this is his own refuge and will be able to retire there for shelter.

After the puppy has had a sleep he will be ready to explore his new surroundings. Immediately he wakes take him out to relieve himself. However clean the puppy has become in his old home, for the first few weeks you will have to reinforce his early training. Remember if the puppy

(OPP) It is essential to have a garden thoroughly fenced, a puppy can find the smallest hole and disappear through it!

A 'Westie' can make an excellent family companion, but children should be taught at a very young age to respect the dog.

makes any mistake and wets or messes inside the house it is your fault and not the puppy's. He will rely on you to get him into a routine and to brainwash him into clean habits. This is why it is essential to be with the new puppy; a person who is out of the house for long periods of time will find it extremely difficult to house-train a puppy as it is constant repetition which will strengthen the habit to be clean. Always put the puppy into the garden immediately he awakes or he has finished eating. Once he has performed in the required place, praise him and make a lot of fuss of him. If a mistake has been made and it does seem too late, still put him out at once. Clean the spot and disinfect well so that he is not attracted to the same spot again.

You will soon become aware of the signs that your puppy is wanting to relieve himself. He will become more active and will move very quickly in circles with his nose to the ground and it becomes obvious that he is looking for 'the correct spot'. Pick him up at once and take him into the garden, it may take several minutes for him to realise why he has been moved but be patient and praise him when results have been achieved.

When the puppy has to be left for a period of time, place newspaper in his puppy pen and he will use that. Sometimes if newspapers are used in the house to house-train a puppy it can be rather difficult to get him to use the garden. He will go out into the garden then immediately come into the house and onto the newspaper to relieve himself. If this happens it may help to put the newspaper outside and hold it in place by a few bricks. After a time place soil on the paper and hopefully this will give the smell of the garden and he should get the idea of going out to relieve himself.

As soon as the dog has relieved himself in the garden the mess should be removed as it can soon become offensive. There are several ways of dealing with the problem. The easiest is to scoop up the waste and flush it down the toilet. There are also available on the market specially made 'dog loos'. These may be very good in soil that is well drained but I have not found them very satisfactory. Another method would be to have a covered bucket with some water and portable toilet fluid in it, waste matter could be put into this to be disposed of at a later time. Personally I think the sooner it is disposed of the better.

Now would be a good time to mention the fact that, although the puppy will not be allowed out at the moment, the time will come when he goes out for walks and relieves himself outside. It is now considered good and

A young dog, just six months old and showing much promise for his future in the show ring. Here he is learning to stand on the table for the judge to assess him.

responsible dog ownership to clean up after your dog. You should carry a small polythene bag and tissues with you, this makes clearing up easier and the bag can be disposed of in a bin specially designed for the purpose or taken home. In many parts of Great Britain this is now becoming compulsory.

In connection with responsible dog ownership and your new puppy, it is as well to stick to a code which makes life for you, your dog and people with whom you come into contact, a much happier one.

1. Keep your dog under control at all times and always keep him on a lead when anywhere near a road or where there are farm animals.

2. Do not allow your dog to foul public places or children's play areas; if he does, clear it up.

3. Do not allow your dog to be noisy. Stop continual barking and keep him quiet at night and in the early morning. Then if he does bark you and your neighbours will realise something is wrong and he will become an asset to everyone.

It is some form of protection for you if, during the first forty-eight hours that you have the puppy, you pay a visit to the vet of your choice. He will be able to give the puppy a general health check. You should have received a puppy from the breeder which has been thoroughly wormed but the vet will probably ask you how often this has been done and when the puppy was last wormed. In the event of there being any doubt you will be given another lot of tablets with which to worm the puppy. Today's medicines are mild and do not require that the puppy be starved at all, so there should be no ill-effect.

Whilst at the vet's he will be able to tell you about inoculation against all the common dog ailments and at what age he recommends them to be done. Some inoculations may be started at eight weeks but it is unlikely that your puppy will be fully protected before he reaches fourteen weeks of age and he should be kept in your own house and garden until your vet tells you it is safe to take him out.

Meanwhile he can be receiving some early basic training at home.

It is never too early to get a puppy used to a collar and lead or a show lead but the puppy should never be dragged around on a lead. To begin with it should be treated as a game. Put on a very soft collar or show lead and let the puppy lead you around the garden, treat the training as a game and only let it last for short periods at a time. If you have another dog he may join in the fun and lead the young puppy around but you must never loose your temper. Simple obedience can also be taught, getting the puppy to come to you when called and not running away is a useful start. Call the puppy to you and when he comes make much of him, telling him how clever he is; if this exercise is repeated several times the puppy will soon get used to coming for praise and attention. Never run after the puppy, they can run faster than you and only think that it is a game – a bad habit that it will take some time to get him out of.

You should also make up your mind as to how you wish your puppy to behave in the house. At this age it is not possible for them to get into a chair unassisted. If you do not wish him to get on a chair at a later stage do not pick him up and put him on the chair next to you but make him stay on the floor. If you intend to restrict him to certain areas of the house, start as you mean to go on and don't expect him to learn the hard way. Never feed your puppy at the table whilst you are eating, it is very annoying to be pestered for food while you are eating.

As soon as you are able to take your puppy out you should take him for short rides in the car. Never just take him out to the vet but for enjoyable walks in the country, he will soon look forward to going for a ride in the car. Never leave your dog in the car in summer, as even with the windows open it can very soon become like a furnace and the dog will quickly die. During the past few years this has been reported in the dog press on several occasions. It is helpful at this stage to have someone else travelling in the car because the puppy should be taught to sit quietly in the rear. If you wish you can buy a dog guard but as a small puppy you may find that he can squeeze through this and extra netting may have to be added. Another option is a dog crate. Most people who show their dogs use a dog box or crate of some type, as most people carry several dogs at the same time. To get a dog used to a crate is a good idea and has several advantages over the fixed dog guard. It means that the car windows can be opened wide in hot weather without danger to the dog, also car doors can be opened with safety. If you are staying in a hotel where dogs are welcome, the crate can be used as temporary kennels in the bedroom whilst you go to meals. If someone enters the room while you are away there is no danger of him running out to find you. There may be other times and places where a pet owner would find a crate useful. It is not cruel as you will find that a 'Westie' loves to go into a small space like this through choice and it becomes his den.

Begin daily grooming with your puppy, making it last for a few minutes only. Place him on a firm table and using a wire brush or terrier pad, brush thoroughly all over. Pay particular attention to the inside of the legs and under the tummy. Do not allow your puppy to chew the brush or you, and even at this stage you must insist that he stands quietly. If he thinks that by misbehaving at this early stage he will be left alone, you will never be able to deal with his coat properly. Whilst the puppy is on the table it is a good

Celtic Song (Britta) at just 6 months.

And again at 10 months, after gaining her Junior Warrant. It is interesting to note that amongst other things she developed a greater depth of chest.

Ch. Crinan Celtic Song aged 22 months. It is interesting to note from the previous two photographs how she developed from the age of six months.

idea to get him used to having his teeth and mouth inspected. Both show dog and pet will benefit by this as a show dog will have to show his teeth at every show and a pet may need to be given medicine or have his teeth inspected by the vet.

After a time where discipline is expected, it is good to have a period of play with your puppy. There are many nice toys on the market but as is often the case with children, simple home-made toys are often best. Small balls and plastic toys are too easily chewed up and swallowed. The middle of a toilet roll is a good toy for a small puppy but I have found the most enjoyable toy for a puppy is a pair of ladies' tights stuffed with a piece of newspaper and tied at intervals in knots, or a sock treated in a similar way will give hours of pleasure. I would not give a puppy an old slipper to play with because it is very difficult for the puppy to differentiate between that and your new pair! Whatever the toy, examine it at regular intervals and if there are small pieces becoming detached, throw the toy away and start again from scratch. Bones too can cause great entertainment and are very good for the teeth but great care should be taken with their choice. Your butcher should be asked for part of a shinbone from a cow. This should be sawn into pieces and not chopped. Chopping would cause dangerous

It is wise to check the teeth of a puppy regularly whilst he is teething. Although this is an excellent mouth of large teeth the puppy has retained a 'puppy canine tooth' which has to be removed by the vet. If left in place it may well spoil the bite of the dog.

splinters which would injure the puppy. A large piece is better than a small one. I have often had an entire bone for the puppies, they will gnaw away happily for hours.

Puppies are great chewers and will pick up and mouth anything that takes their fancy. They can be particularly interested in stones and pebbles in the garden and you should be continually on the watch for this. Carefully remove the stone or other article from the puppy's mouth, telling him 'no' at the same time. As soon as he gives up his prize, praise him. In this way he will soon get used to giving you anything he has been holding in his mouth.

Having spent a lot of money on purchasing the puppy, you must be prepared to spend a good deal of time and perhaps more money in looking after him. If you are at all unsure about the health of your puppy, seek the advice of a vet without delay. A puppy can go downhill very quickly and you should not put off a visit to the vet if the puppy is at all unwell. A quick visit could save days of suffering and a long climb back to health. Having bought a healthy puppy, do everything you can to keep him that way.

5 Feeding

As I mentioned before, when taking home your new puppy it is important to stick to the diet recommended by the breeder but you may decide that you would like to change it. If this is the case always do so carefully and a little at a time so as to give as little a shock to the system as possible. When feeding your youngster try to stick to the same time for meals each day.

You should make sure that whatever the age of your 'Westie', it has a sound balanced diet with all the vitamins and minerals necessary for good health. At one time it used to be the case that the conscientious breeder would add large amounts of extra vitamins and other additives to the diet, but it is more important to give a good wholesome diet as an excess of vitamins is wasteful and can sometimes be dangerous. Basically dogs need

Ch. Erisort Sleighbelle

food for growth and to replace tissue, also to maintain body functions. There are more specialist needs required by puppies, growing youngsters, stud dogs and pregnant and lactating bitches. Also older dogs may need a change of diet to keep them fit and healthy.

The food can be broken down into three main areas, these are carbohydrates, proteins and fats. Carbohydrates supply the largest portion of energy but if eaten in excess of the body's needs, will cause fatness. Proteins are necessary for healthy growth of the body and can be found in such food as meat, offal, fish, eggs and milk. Fat is a rich source of energy which is needed to keep the dog in peak condition. The amount needed by the dog will vary according to the time of year. In cold weather more fat will be consumed by the dog's body than in very warm weather. Therefore, a dog's diet should be adjusted to suit the time of year, the age of the dog and his role in life.

Vitamins and minerals are needed by a dog in his diet but if the dog is maintained on a wholesome balanced diet most of his needs will be found in that. Vitamin A helps to fight infection and vitamin D is essential for the body to absorb calcium and phosphorus but an excess of this could cause problems as it must be balanced with the amount of calcium and phosphorus to be used correctly. Vitamin C and vitamin B are essential and can be found in meat, liver, yeast and dairy products although they can be killed by cooking and by eating raw egg white, so raw egg whites should never be fed to a dog. Vitamin E is essential for reproduction and muscle tone and is found in wholemeal products. It is sometimes given to stud dogs when they are being used more than usual at stud and for working dogs. Vitamin K is essential for the correct clotting of the blood and is given by the vet in injection form in massive doses as an antidote to Warfarin and snake bites. Trace elements and minerals are also necessary and can be found in the well balanced diet but apart from specific times these are all found in the adequate diet.

Young puppies can be given small amounts of added vitamins and there are many proprietary brands on the market, but it is important not to add too much to the food as this could be worse than nothing at all. Sterilized bone flour can be purchased from the vet and is an excellent source of calcium for the growing puppy and pregnant and lactating bitches (see chapter on breeding for more details).

For the majority of pet owners the most common way to feed a dog is the use of tinned dog food and a glance at the label will show that the meat also contains the necessary additives for a normal healthy adult dog. Tinned meat needs to be fed with care as too much can upset the tummy of a dog. I have found that one third of a tin (395g) is enough per meal with mixer

Pillerton Pearl

Ch. Backmuir Sweetbriar

for an adult West Highland although this may need some adjustment according to the size and activeness of your dog. Many tins of food suggest a much larger intake than this, and of course feeding a puppy is different as he will need several small meals rather than one large one (see chapter on rearing a litter). If you find you wish to feed tinned food, find one that suits your dog and stick to that as some types may cause him tummy upsets.

There are types of dog food which look like biscuits and are called 'complete' food. They include all the essential elements that a dog needs. It is only necessary to have available a bowl of fresh cold water, as this diet is fed dry and the dog should be allowed free access to water to balance the dryness of the food. It is a very convenient way to feed a dog but I have never found my own dogs to show much interest in this method of feeding, although I have seen other dogs, obviously in superb condition, fed solely on 'complete' dog food.

Fresh meat can be fed raw or lightly cooked and the stock produced by this can be used to soak the meal beforehand. Types of meat that can be used are ox meat or shin beef although this is now rather expensive and liver could be added in small amounts to the diet but care should be taken when feeding offal as too much would cause the dog's motions to become very loose indicating that the food is too rich. All the above of course are red meats and white meat is an excellent source of meat for the dog, especially those having to be kept on a light diet for reasons of illness or other specific reasons. Chicken, if it is frozen, should be well thawed for the same reason as when feeding to humans and it is possible to buy hens which are usually much stronger in flavour and cheaper than chicken. If the meat is removed from the bone whilst hot it cuts down the waste and the bones are easier to remove. Remember that chicken bones should never, under any circumstances, be fed to a dog. They are very brittle and could cause injury to the dog during the digestion process.

Fish is also very acceptable as an alternative to red or white meat and is very useful as a change for puppies as they sometimes get rather bored with the same taste. Sometime you will find that an older dog will be able to digest the fish more easily than meat and it is good for them but do remember to go through the fish thoroughly with your fingers before feeding to your 'Westie'. Fish bones, being almost transparent, are very difficult to spot and it is essential to remove them all as they are as dangerous as chicken bones when swallowed.

All dogs from time to time will eat grass and as this is indigestible it will make them sick, so it is a good idea to feed raw cabbage and carrots. My dogs cannot resist carrots and seem to know when I am about to prepare them for myself. They love a stick of carrot to chew. As well as being good for them, the carrots help to keep the teeth clean and if you feel that it is better, small amounts of raw carrot and cabbage can be grated and mixed with their food.

These are only a few suggestions about the use of various foodstuffs. Breeders will have their own pet fads and theories about what to feed and how to feed it and much can be learnt by listening to them. All types of food have their merits and disadvantages. Whatever you choose, remember that the better your dog is nourished, the better he will look and feel.

6 Grooming

Care and grooming of the 'Westie' coat should begin as soon as possible and it should be a pleasurable experience for both dog and owner.

Before even thinking about grooming, it is essential to look at the coat of the adult West Highland. When seen to perfection a show or pet dog should have a well groomed, tidy look about it without looking overdone. Stripping should not be taken to excess or else your 'Westie' would be in danger of looking more like a Wire Fox Terrier. There is an increasing tendency for this to be seen in the ring at the moment and newcomers would do well to read the breed standard, for it states there that there should be a two-inch coat. It is much harder to keep a good longer coat in condition than a very short one and this is possibly the reason for its increase.

The coat of the West Highland should be thick and weatherproof. It consists of two layers. The outer one is hard and wiry, in some dogs almost like coconut matting. It has a silvery whiteness to it and next to a Sealyham a 'Westie' will not look very clean because of this type of whiteness. If this coat is parted, it is possible to see the second coat underneath. This is usually whiter and is very soft and fluffy and is called the undercoat. These two coats make up the 'double' coat of the West Highland as called for in the breed standard.

It is very important for the beginner in the breed and the owner of a new puppy to understand about grooming both coats. It is very easy to think that you are grooming the coat thoroughly when in fact you are merely brushing the surface.

Tools and equipment for grooming

Tables: First let us consider the multitude of tools and equipment available and the best ones for the job. Before thinking about the tools themselves, it is important to consider where you are going to groom your

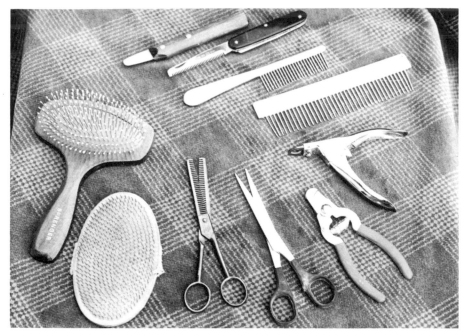

Tools for grooming and coat care.
Anti-clockwise: a pin brush in rubber mounting; terrier pad; thinning scissors; straight bladed scissors; nail clippers; guillotine nail clippers; metal comb; metal comb with handle; stripping knife (pen-knife type); fine stripping knife.

dog. If you are not going to show him you will not want to go to the expense of buying a special table. I would recommend a space on the work bench in the garage as these are usually placed at a suitable height to work at standing up so are ideal for grooming purposes.

As a youngster you may find it difficult to restrain the puppy at the same time as grooming him, so a restraint in the form of a collar and lead can be hung from a suitable shelf or bracket fixed above the table. A word of warning must be given here – never leave your dog with the collar around his neck not even for a second or you will find that it will become like a hangman's noose. The wood of the bench may be rather shiny and so it is better to cover it with either a spare piece of carpet or a piece of rubber – a car mat is ideal for the purpose.

If you intend showing, you will need a portable table. These can be very expensive and it is wise to look at the many different styles available and to see what other people are using and ask their opinions before purchasing one of your own. There are two main types. The first is just a table and my own preference is to have a lightweight aluminium one with folding tubular legs. The work surface being just big enough on which to stand your dog and easily portable, they are fine for use at small shows where space can be very limited or at the larger shows around the ringside. If this is the type you choose you will also need to have a separate trolley to move all your gear to the benches or grooming area. The second type of table would do away with this necessity as there are wheels rather like those on a supermarket trolley, attached to the underneath of the table. The grooming surface would measure something like 24 inches by 30 inches (.6m by .8m). When used in its other mode as a trolley this will be ample on which to fit either two crates, side by side, or even four if a second layer is made. The trolley table is fitted with either a rope or a handle with which to pull it along. If using a portable table it is necessary to have a grooming support. These can be purchased separately or in some more elaborate tables they are incorporated into the table.

Next to the tools, and the most important one is yours for free. That is your fingers. Use these as much as you can and your dog's coat will look far better. A scissored coat can look very hard and objectionable.

Brushes: Brushes are the next thing to look at. The one normally available in pet shops and bought by novice owners is not really suitable for this breed. It is double sided, having bristles on one side and wire pins on the reverse side. These are set in a rubber backing and attached to a wooden handle. In fact bristle is no use at all for the coat of the West Highland because it fails to penetrate the hard outer coat. The best available brush is perhaps the simplest but unless you go to a dog show or have a particularly good pet shop you may have difficulty in finding one. Ask your local pet shop to order one for you because they are readily available to them. They are known as terrier pads and consist of an oval-shaped red rubber pad which is covered on one side with short steel pins. The rubber pad is not mounted onto wood but the handle is formed out of a piece of webbing which is sewn into the rubber. Because the rubber is pliable it can be moulded to the shape of the dog's body making knot removal and general brushing much easier.

As well as the terrier pad many people have a wooden-backed one, again make sure that the pins are set onto a rubber back. It is also advisable to have ball points as this will enable you to groom right through both coats to the skin without any danger of sticking the points into the dog. I find this type of brush very useful for the more general everyday grooming. Another type of brush that is frequently seen is a small rectangular brush with bent metal bristles set into a rubber base which is mounted into wood with an angled handle. Care must be exercised in using a brush of this type because the pins are very fine and set close together and this has the tendency to pull out large amounts of undercoat thus leaving your dog with a single coat. One more brush that you would find extremely useful is a small nail brush. This is used only for applying chalk to the coat when grooming but is unlikely to penetrate through to the skin.

A much loved pet. His quality is evident but he would be much improved if his coat was stripped correctly.

Combs: It is a good idea to have several good quality metal combs as you will find that they are suitable for different purposes. Personally I find two useful. One comb has teeth along its entire length and has long teeth all the same distance apart. Some people prefer a metal comb with shorter teeth which are close at one end and more widely spaced at the other. My other comb has finer teeth and a handle of metal. When buying a comb it is better to choose those made entirely of metal because those made with plastic handles or plastic moulded to look like horn, may look very attractive but are unsuitable if it becomes necessary to sterilize the comb at any time in boiling water. This would probably loosen the metal shank inside the plastic, making the comb unusable.

Stripping Knives: The term 'knife' is misleading and should be disregarded. The so-called 'knife' should never be used to cut the coat but merely as an aid to those with weak fingers, to enable them to grip the coat better prior to pulling from the roots. There should be no evidence of hair that has been cut on a correctly groomed West Highland. Therefore, the sharpness of the 'knife' is not something you should test but its ability to grip the coat. Again I find two types of use. The first has teeth widely set apart and is used on the back of the dog or where more coat is left, the second is finer and is useful for use on the neck and shoulders. My coarse knife is hand made and I would be lost without it but there are commercially available knives made of similar standard. These have a short blade approximately $1\frac{1}{2}$ inches (3.8cm) long and are set into a handle of wood. My other 'knife' takes the form of a penknife having two blades, one coarse the other fine. This is extremely useful as it can be carried easily in the pocket. I would not recommend the type of knife widely available and distinguished by the fact that it has a sharp blade screwed onto the side of a short metal comb. This has a tendency to leave an obvious cut to the coat.

Scissors: Scissors must be used with discretion. You will find that on some types of coat you will need to use them more frequently than on others. You will need to have both thinning and plain bladed scissors. Thinning scissors come in two main types. Those with teeth on both blades and the type with one toothed blade and one straight blade. Within the two different types there are also different numbers of teeth on each blade. I prefer the type with both blades toothed and with a large number of teeth. These are less likely to leave an obvious mark on the coat but you should still exercise great care in their use.

Plain bladed scissors are also available in straight and curved blades and you should have one of each pair. Also a small pair of straight scissors with round points are very useful to trim around and in between the dog's pads. Always buy good quality scissors as they will hold their edge much longer.

Grooming powders and shampoos: There are several types of dry white powder available on the market sold under different trade names. The idea behind them is to dry clean the coat. Calcium carbonate is the usual type of chalk used by exhibitors. It can be purchased from the chemist in its pure form where it forms the basis of medicine to soothe the stomach. Another form of calcium carbonate that can be bought is not as white or as fine as the first type and it is used in the production of whiting. It is as good as the first type but not quite so easy to remove from the coat. Magnesium carbonate can also be used but is much lighter in block form and will rub freely off the block unlike calcium carbonate in block form.

Shampoos are available in wide varieties. For general use a medicated insecticidal shampoo may be the most suitable. Care should be taken when choosing a shampoo for show dogs as they may contravene the regulations about coat preparation.

Apart from the tools, chalk and shampoo mentioned above, there are a few other things that you will need to keep your dog well groomed. A nail clipper is vital to keep your dog's nails short. Different types are available but 'Westies' have such strong, thick nails that I find the one working on the guillotine principle to be the easiest to use. To finish off the nail a large file of the type used by woodworkers can be used.

It is wise to have available a good flea spray as even the cleanest pet can sometimes have unwelcome visitors and they are best dealt with immediately they are noticed. I also like to use a spray to condition and refresh the coat when doing day-to-day grooming.

Now that you have a suitable place and materials to groom your dog it should be a daily procedure. It need take only a few minutes to groom the dog thoroughly from head to tail.

Grooming a puppy

Daily grooming should be done with firm control for it would be all too easy for a puppy to wriggle and fall off the surface on which you are grooming. This may do serious damage so make sure the puppy is held securely at all times.

First make the puppy stand quietly on the table and reassure him by stroking and talking to him. Do not let him fight you even if in a playful manner nor snap and chew at the brush for this will become a bad habit which will be hard to break. The best tool that you have for more general grooming of the puppy would be your terrier pad. All parts of the puppy must be brushed daily to keep the coat and skin in healthy condition. It is when grooming that you will be likely to spot the beginnings of a problem which, if left, may be much more difficult to treat.

Begin by brushing the puppy's tummy. Carefully hold him by the front legs, holding them a little way off the table surface but with his hind legs still on the table and quickly brush from his front to his rear legs. Do not be too firm in your brushing because the hair on the back of the tummy between the back legs is rather thin and care must be taken not to scratch the skin itself. After having done this, lower the puppy gently onto the table surface and insist that he stands quietly again before you continue with the grooming process. Next do the front legs. Pick up each front leg separately and hold the paw firmly. Take the terrier pad and starting at the armpits, brush the hair first in the upwards direction down to and including the paw and then in the direction of the growth of the coat. Make sure the whole of the leg has been brushed in this way, checking particularly the thicker areas of hair behind the elbows. Now brush the hind legs in a similar fashion but here you may not find it necessary to lift the paw off the table surface. If you do care must be taken not to pull the puppy off balance as he may lose confidence.

Next groom the head. Start with the muzzle and the area under the chin. Firstly brush the hair flat against the skin, checking that it is free from knots, then carefully brush the area between the eyes taking care not to stick the pins in the eyes. At the same time as grooming around the eyes, clean any particles of dust out of the corners that may have gathered since the day before's grooming. Also make sure that there are no hairs curling up and touching the surface of the eye, as this can cause them to water. This tends to happen when the puppy's coat is of a certain length. A small amount of grease can be used to keep it in place until the hair has grown. If the puppy's eyes seem to produce too much secretion your vet's opinion should be sought. Now brush the top of the head and around the ears. Check that the ears are clean and free from any unpleasant odour. After

Two of my own dogs as youngsters. They are Ch. Clan Crinan at 10 months and Crinan Count Your Blessings aged 8 months.

having brushed the hair on the head in the direction of growth, brush in the opposite direction so that it stands away from the head. In this way you are starting to train the hair to stand away from the head in the desired 'chrysanthemum' shape.

The last part to be groomed is the body, including the tail. Brush from the chin to the top of the front legs moving around the sides to the shoulders, smooth this part of the coat down as far as possible in the direction in which it grows. Now brush the body, starting from the bottom and working up the sides to the spine and continue up the back of the neck to the ears. Make sure that the areas around the back of the ears and the base of the tail are thoroughly checked as it is here that tangles can start. Brush up the tail from root to tip and finally smooth the hair on the puppy's rear. As you groom check the state of the puppy's skin to make sure that it is clear of blemish and that there are no unwelcome visitors. Using the comb, make a final check on the backs of the legs and down the sides of the body for knots. If you have done the first process thoroughly and daily, the comb should slip through the coat however thick it may be, without encountering any mat or tangle. If, however, a tangle has formed, tease it out gently pulling the mat apart using the point of the comb to ease out the parts nearer the skin.

Done thoroughly the whole of this process should take no more than about ten minutes, although of course this will vary with the age and the amount of coat your puppy has.

The weekly groom

On the weekly groom, more attention should be paid to detail. Every week check your puppy's claws and give him a manicure using either the guillotine cutters or a file. He may still have his dew claws and it is important to keep these short as if they are allowed to grow they will curl round and dig into the pad making walking very painful. Many pet owners take their dogs to a vet to have claws cut but really it should be treated as routine and should be no more difficult than cutting your own nails.

The nail is made up of two parts, the inner living part carrying the blood vessels and called 'the quick' and the outer nail itself. It is most important when cutting the nail that you cut only the outer part because if the quick is cut it will cause bleeding and hurt the puppy. If your puppy has some pink claws the two different parts can easily be seen and from these it is possible to judge how much to cut from the black ones. Cut a little at a time, if necessary just taking off a small amount at the end. You will soon be able to judge by the state of the nail, when to stop.

When checking the nails, run your finger between the pads and check that no foreign bodies are trapped in between them. In summer it is quite possible for a dog to pick up small pieces of grit covered in tar and these become lodged in the hair of the pad. Using a small pair of sharp round-ended scissors, trim the hair from between the pads, this will also prevent uncomfortable mats of hair from forming.

Having done daily and weekly grooming on a regular basis, you will have a clean, knot-free puppy willing to stand and behave as he will know that he is not going to be hurt and sure that he will please you.

Your puppy's coat will, however, all the time be growing longer and thicker and before too many weeks have passed you should be thinking seriously about keeping the coat to a manageable length.

Keeping the puppy coat tidy

Tidying the puppy coat should be a slow and gradual process which should be incorporated into the daily and weekly grooming plan.

Before discussing this in more detail, let us look at the alternative. You may have decided that you yourself do not want to be responsible for the more major item of stripping. This does not mean, however, that grooming should be left undone. It is extremely cruel to your pet to leave him ungroomed for weeks or months in the hope that when he is stripped he will look like a well kept specimen of the breed. He will no doubt feel very irritable and make life extremely difficult for the person you have selected to do the 'hairdressing' on your dog. I have often said to someone with a dog in this condition 'Would you ever dream of going to the hairdresser with your own hair in that condition?' You go to have your hair styled and shaped so that you look more attractive to others or for a special event but between visits you look after your hair daily. You should treat your dog in the same way and feel thoroughly ashamed of a tangled and knotty West Highland.

When purchasing your West Highland you should try to find out the name and address of someone local to you who can maintain a terrier coat in the correct manner. This means hand stripping and not clipping. Many people have taken their 'Westie' to be 'trimmed' only to find when he is returned to them that all his coat has been taken off with electric clippers and he ends up looking like a little pig rather than a rough-coated terrier. Beware and make sure that your 'Westie' is hand stripped. Apart from looking unacceptable, when a dog is clipped the roots of dead hair are left in the skin and this can lead to scratching and skin trouble. 'A Westie' that has dead hair removed correctly is less likely to have trouble, so it is wise to spend time and trouble in searching out someone who can be recommended to deal with the coat correctly. When you have found someone they may recommend to you the intervals at which your dog should be stripped. This will take into account his type of coat and the best way to keep it in condition. A dog can be kept in coat throughout the year. It is wrong to think that a coat needs to be long and thick in winter and short and thin in summer.

The correct coat of a West Highland acts as insulation suitable for the coldest weather and the hottest summer's day. The undercoat, resembling fur, traps the air, this would act in summer to keep the body cool and in winter warm. The outer coat is waterproof so helps in the process and also helps to keep the dog dry, so a quick towelling after a walk in the rain and his undercoat and skin should be dry and clean. To subject a West Highland to an extremely short hair cut in the height of summer would be wrong. The skin would become visible through the jacket and your dog could well become affected by the heat or even suffer from sun-stroke.

Some may be willing to attempt the process of stripping themselves. The basic principle involved in this is simplicity itself, what is more difficult and seldom seen to perfection is the presentation of a dog in immaculate show condition. But let us start with the basics and learn from the beginning so that you grow more experienced as your dog grows his adult coat.

The process of hand stripping is not cruel because it merely involves gripping a few of the longer dead hairs firmly between your thumb and index finger and by a quick downward jerk of the wrist, removing them. It is easier if the other hand (if you are right handed this would be the left hand) is used to hold still the rest of the coat and skin. Always pull out the

FIG 20 Hand stripping. Grasp a few hairs at a time and with a sharp downward movement remove the hair.

FIG 21 Showing varying lengths of coat to be left on a dog and its direction of growth.

FIG 22 Effect of different amounts of hair to overall shape of dog.

It is interesting to note how exactly the same shape of dog (dotted line) can be made to look entirely different by the amount of hair left on the dog in different places
(1) Looks shorter and longer in the leg.
(2) The head is bigger in proportion to the body and the body looks much heavier.

old coat in the direction in which you want the new coat to lie. Do not attempt to remove more than a few hairs at a time. With practice you will soon find this an easy process.

With a young puppy therefore the idea is to remove the wispy puppy coat a little at a time, the aim being to tidy the coat and as it grows, gradually develop the shape of the adult coat. You will find that your puppy, if it has not had any of its coat removed at all, will be more untidy in some places than in others. If we move from front to back and look at each point in turn, these will be as follows.

The head: It is unlikely that the head itself will grow very much hair although there may be very long wispy hairs that can be removed at about eight weeks old if the puppy's coat is relatively soft. At about three to four months old the original puppy coat will have grown quite thin and another coat will be obvious below this and now is the time to start removing the old coat. Do be careful if you want to start showing your puppy at six months old, you will find that coat on head and legs grows extremely slowly so take only a few hairs at a time or else the puppy will be very short of hair on his head in his early show appearances.

The ears are the part of the head that need the most constant attention. Even as early as four or five weeks old they can be receiving their first tidy. In a very young puppy, I prefer to trim the tops with scissors but the purist would frown upon this, preferring to use the finger and thumb method at all times. Take only the long hair from the upper part of the ear. You will notice that it seems that the ears of a puppy look very large but after the removal of excess hair they will look small and very neat.

Neck and shoulders: I think the neck and shoulders of a puppy are the parts that, when trimmed, make most difference to the appearance of a young puppy. Stand your puppy on the table and groom the coat, you will probably find what can be described as a ruff running from behind the ears to the front point of the shoulder blades. Remove this slowly, pulling a few hairs at a time. If the puppy objects, it may be that the hair is not ready to come out. In this case leave it a little longer and try again in a few days. As well as the ruff, there will be long hair at the top of the neck where it joins the jaw. This must be shortened. Most dogs are rather tender at this point and it would be better to use thinning scissors or a stripping knife. Removing the ruff and hair on the front of the neck will begin to show up the head as an area with longer coat. Where the skull joins the spine behind the ears the longer bits of coat can be removed with finger and thumb.

Front legs: Look at these from the front to begin with. You should remove any hair at the elbows which sticks out of line from the majority of the leg hair, this can also be viewed from the side. Then use a pair of straight scissors and tidy around the foot, not right up to the pads themselves but to make the paw look neat and round.

Back legs and area below tail: The hind feet should be tidied in the same way as the front feet. Looking from the back of the puppy small amounts of hair can be removed from areas around the hips, but remember this does grow very slowly. The area below the tail should be as short as possible gradually blending into longer hair at the hocks. Remove any long wisps to encourage the hair to grow thickly on the legs. If allowed to grow unchecked, leg hair will become very long and sparse.

Back, sides and tail: The back can be shortened quite considerably, as on the adult dog this is always kept shorter than the sides of the dog. New growth needs to be encouraged so as soon as a dead hair or a long piece of coat appears out of place it should be stripped out. The shorter back should be blended into the longer side coat and skirt. The tail should be the shape of an upturned carrot, thick at the base terminating in a point.

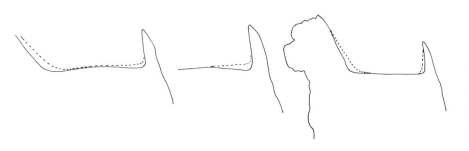

FIG 23 (*Left*) Correcting an uneven topline by building up hair at the shoulders and at the top of the rump.

FIG 24 (*Centre*)Improving a low-set tail.

FIG 25 Improving the look of an upright shoulder which is making the back look overlong. Hair can be left behind the neck and a little in front of the tail.

Any fringe on the puppy tail at the back and the point should be stripped away to encourage a hard short coat to grow in its place.

The main aim should be to encourage the growth of coat in the correct places and the removal of long coat where it is not wanted. Some assessment can be made of the puppy's good and bad points as it is important to be able in good presentation to accentuate the good and as far as possible disguise the bad. It is no use being blind to your puppy's faults and being offended when they are pointed out to you by other people.

Brushing the adult dog

This is almost the same as grooming a puppy. The coat is much thicker and will therefore take longer to groom thoroughly. Go over the coat in the same order as with the puppy, starting with the underbelly. You will probably find that you have to make more use of the comb because you are more likely to have knots in a heavy adult coat. If you have a male, shorten any hair that is likely to become heavily stained and give him a rinse in clean water to prevent him from becoming smelly. Some dogs may need to be washed down daily, others only on more infrequent occasions.

Using the terrier pad brush through the head checking the small folds on either side of the lower jaw. It is here that the coat has a tendency to become stained and there can be eczema present. It is best to remove the stained coat either by pulling it out or by cutting it close to the roots. This

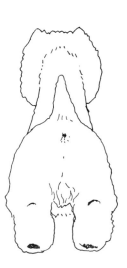

FIG 26 The shape to be aimed at when looking at the dog from the rear.

FIG 27 Front view: *Left* stripped and *right* in its unstripped condition.

will prevent the stain from becoming more widespread. After brushing, comb through the beard to make sure that the coat is free from knots. Many West Highlands, having eaten their meal, will rub their chin on the grass or carpet, cleaning any excess of food from their whiskers but the process does seem to encourage the formation of knots.

The neck, shoulder and body can be treated in a similar manner. At certain times of the year you will notice that large amounts of the soft furry coat underneath come out in the grooming process. This is unfortunate if you are showing the dog as the coat seems to become open. However, if it was loose enough to come out in a terrier pad it was better that it came out as it will grow back more quickly once removed. This can happen in a sudden warm spell, in the middle of winter or when a bitch has been in season. It will also happen when she has nursed a litter of puppies. You will probably find that her outer jacket becomes a little worse for wear as well. A bitch having her first litter seems to be affected more than with subsequent litters.

Complete the thorough groom by thoroughly combing the legs and tail and checking through the pads as in the puppy.

7 Stripping and Show Preparation

So far instruction for general grooming has been for someone owning a dog for the first time and needing a grounding in basic grooming techniques. It may be that the puppy you bought is turning into a rather nice specimen of the breed and you have decided that it would be an interesting hobby to show the dog.

Before getting to the showing stage, you may have hours of work ahead of you over several months, for a good show coat and shape are not arrived at in one grooming session but over a period of time and many short sessions. Between these periods, long periods can be spent in assessing the dog and deciding where to take off coat in a future grooming period. If this technique of presentation is used, a dog can be kept in show coat for the majority of the year. It is more difficult for the bitch for the reasons I have already mentioned.

Let us start from the beginning, presuming that you have been grooming your dog thoroughly and removing the obvious dead coat from his jacket. The first session is going to be one of more mammoth proportions as in some areas you will have large amounts of coat to remove. The idea to begin with is to get some idea of shape into the dog's coat. In doing this you may find that you lose all the topcoat in some areas. You should not be expecting to show a dog whose coat has been allowed to get into this condition, for several months. Where you start stripping is largely a personal choice but I prefer to begin with the neck, shoulders and top line.

Divide the hair on a line between the ears; the hair in front of this line to be treated as head and behind as neck. Starting at this point start to strip out the very long and rather bushy hair. An application of chalk may make it easier for you to grip the hair. Your aim should be to grade the coat from very short at ear level, gradually lengthening until the point of the shoulder blades is reached. This strip of coat should be quite narrow at its highest point and go wider at the base. At the same time, for it is impossible to think of any part of the body in isolation, hair should be stripped from the sides of the neck and shoulders, gradually blending the shoulders into the longer coat at the junction of the shoulder blades.

The short area of the sides of the neck should extend underneath the chin, thus giving a shorter frame to the longer coat on the head and should reach as far as the breast bone. The top line of the dog is extremely important and care should be taken to keep it level. By leaving the hair on the base of the neck slightly longer than the junction of the neck and skull, it is possible to lengthen the look of the neck and considerably shorten the back. Make the dog stand and try to merge the neck hair into the top line. You should try to stand your dog so that you are looking at him in a mirror. This will give you the judge's view of him and you will soon get used to seeing what needs to be removed from the top line. The coat, when at its peak, should be rather dense and about 2 inches (51mm) long but a careful examination of the coat will show that there are hairs of many lengths. Some new coat, just growing, some the correct length and other pieces which are obviously past their best and are ready to come out but in this way it is possible to keep your dog in good coat condition for a long time.

The skirt on the sides of the dog will need to be tidied considerably. View your dog from the rear, especially on the move, and see what is visible to you. If you are able to detect the forelegs they will need to have hair removed from the sides and in particular from the area around the elbows. Hair on the sides of the dog may be sticking out, giving him rather a barrel shape and this needs to be neatened up to give his sides a flatter appearance. Although it is nice to see a West Highland with good furnishing it should be possible to see daylight underneath him. It is foreign to the breed to have a coat that sweeps the floor when the dog is moving. If the skirt furnishings are on the thin side, it does help to take a fraction off the longer hairs with the straight scissors, do not however cut the whole line of the skirt because this will give too hard a line. The rump of the dog should be stripped as a continuation of the back. Do not leave a greater amount of coat on the flanks as this has the visual effect of lengthening the dog and this should be avoided. As mentioned earlier it should not be possible to see past the hindquarters. If the shoulders of the dog are rather too bulky it may be necessary to leave a little extra coat on the rear of the dog.

After dealing with the front and middle sections of the dog and his flanks, look next at the shape of the hind legs and, with your knowledge of the breed standard in mind, strip and trim the hocks to accentuate their correct shape. Remember that viewed from the rear the hocks should be parallel. Also get someone to move the dog so that you can see how he looks moving away from you. It may be necessary to adjust your stripping technique to improve a point. Tidy up the pads of the dog but do not cut too close to them around the sides, you should aim to make them round when the foot is lifted. When the dog moves away from you this will completely expose the largest of the pads. Both from the side and the rear, the hind leg should be trimmed to give a good bend of stifle.

Next to the tail and rear. The tail is thicker at the base than at the point and this should be emphasized by leaving thicker hair at the base of the tail, thinning and shortening it to the point where any excess hair being longer than the tip of the tail can be removed by careful stripping and trimming. If the tail itself has little natural taper this can be adapted by carefully leaving more hair on the base of the tail. At the junction of the tail and back it may be necessary to take some hair from the back to enable the tail to sit properly into the top line without disturbing it. The rear should be presented as flat as possible, having the visual effect of shortening the dog, also improving his shape. However take care, as to take too much especially at the sides of the tail can give it a low-set appearance. The hair on the upper rear should be as short as possible and thinning scissors will probably have to be used as the dog is rather tender around this part of his anatomy. As you move down the rear the hair should be left a little longer thus giving a nice rounded appearance and also blending in with the upper part of the hind legs. The hair covering the testicles or the vulva should be neatened up a little with scissors.

The head is the crowning glory of the West Highland and is usually left until last as it can help to balance the whole of the dog. If too much hair is removed from the head the whole of the proportion of the dog may be ruined and as head hair is very slow growing, it will take months to correct. The hair on the head is usually a little softer than that of the body but by constantly removing the longer hairs by hand and without the aid of scissors the texture can be improved. This should be started when the dog is a puppy and not left until the hair on the head has reached the desired length as to start hand stripping at this stage will leave the coat rather sparse. Thoroughly brush the hair on the head and remove, taking a few hairs at a time, any that extend beyond the tips of the ears. The better textured hair is also more likely to stand up in the correct manner, giving rise to the chrysanthemum head. The ear tips should be trimmed if at all possible by hand to remove any fringes from about the top half inch. The back of the ear should also be hand stripped, do not use scissors here. Trim the outer edge of the ears so that they blend in with and become part of, the head furnishings. Do not take too much hair from lower down the ears as it can make them look very large. Take out some hair from the inside of the ear and shorten anything which appears as a tuft on either side of the ear when viewing the head from the front.

The head should be viewed from both sides and the front before a start is made on stripping. If the top of the head and the area between the ears and above the eyes has had regular attention as mentioned earlier, it will need little extra attention to remove excess hair to leave a rounded dome between the ears. This same dome can be viewed from the side between the ears and the stop. The hair on the head should be considerably longer than the hair on the rest of the body and should act as a frame for the West Highland expression. Where the skull joins the muzzle it is necessary to shorten the hair a little, if left the same length it will have the effect of totally obscuring the eyes, although if they are completely uncovered they will look too bold. It is nice to see the dark eyes peering out at you. If done carefully the hair from the muzzle between the eyes can also be shortened and this will give the effect of shortening the muzzle. The sides of the head will also need shortening. If your dog has rather large ears, excess hair left at the sides and jowls will only emphasize them and not make them smaller. Trimming will be necessary under the beard but only to the extent of continuing the round appearance. Some exhibitors seem to have a craze for chopping off virtually the whole of the beard making the West Highland look as though it has no bottom jaw. Some trimming will also be needed under the eyes and on the muzzle. Remember that you want the head to look round from all directions and not just like a dinner plate. As I have already said it is the head that balances the dog. A large dog needs a large head so if the head is too small leave more hair to balance it. If the head is narrow in appearance, the hair on top of the head can be shortened a little and the beard left longer. If most of the beard is removed the head can look rather shallow. The head should have, when complete, a slightly shaggy appearance. A 'Westie' whose head has been cut entirely with scissors can look very smart but the appearance gained is not correct. It can be seen regularly on the heads of 'Westies' in the show ring, the reasons for this type of trimming are usually two-fold. The first is because the dog's hair is woolly and the second is to hide poor bone formation.

By attending shows and watching the preparation of show dogs in progress you can learn a lot about the refinements of grooming. There is no absolute right and wrong way to present a dog, only the one that suits your dog best. Don't be led blindly by the fashion of the day. This form of preparation may suit the top winning dog but it may be entirely unsuitable for your own West Highland.

Cleaning the West Highland

The West Highland has a fairly dry coat and therefore frequent baths to remove excess grease are not necessary. However, it is necessary to have a very clean white dog in the ring. The Kennel Club Regulations insist that all chalk be removed from the coat before the dog is exhibited and that no substance be used which enhances the coat in any way, so the use of bleach is absolutely ruled out and many of the shampoos available on the market today must be suspect as must coat dressings. The K.C. does not say that powdered chalk may not be used but only that it cannot be used within the precincts of the show. Block chalk can, however, be used within the show. This seems to me an impossible rule to keep as chalk is impossible to remove in its entirety and an examination under a microscope would almost without doubt reveal its presence. So great care must be taken to adhere to the K.C. regulations for to flout them could mean disqualification of the dog and the loss of his award and worse still the possible banning of the owner from further competition.

Disguising undesirable faults

No dog is perfect and it may be necessary to try to disguise the more glaring faults although this will never deceive a good judge.

The most important point when preparing your dog's coat for the show ring is to know his faults and accept them for if you are kennel blind you will never make progress in the show ring.

Front legs when stripped to perfection look straight when viewed from the front but it is not unusual for one foot to turn out a little. Leave a little extra hair around the inside of the foot and the outside of the leg a little further up. Care should be taken when dealing with elbows because tufts of hair left on the points of the elbows can accentuate a slightly crooked front, making it look worse. It is possible to correct the look of cow hocks by leaving more hair around the inside of the pad.

Another point where the camouflage of an undesirable fault can help the look of the dog considerably, is the neck and top line of the dog when viewed from the side. If the area around the tail is higher than at the point of the shoulders, the hair in this area can be developed so that the hair becomes thicker. If this area of hair is thick and it gradually becomes thinner to the base of the tail this would help to level out the back. Upright shoulders leading to an overlong top line can be improved by leaving more hair at the base of the neck, gradually blending the hair from the neck to the back. There should be a level back. I am convinced that many sloping top lines are caused by the owner of the dog trying to give the impression of a shorter back and a better shoulder placement. The result of doing this badly shows a slope, starting behind the ears and ending in front of the tail.

If you are trying to disguise a fault it is important only to correct as much as is necessary, to overdo it may develop the look of a worse fault which was not there in the first place.

8 Showing

When buying your West Highland White Terrier you may have thought of nothing else than buying a good quality specimen of the breed as a family companion. Having groomed and trained him to walk well on a lead and seen his personality develop over a number of months, may have made you wonder about the possibilities of showing. You may have gone back to the breeder for help with stripping and have been encouraged by them to enter your dog for a show.

Before entering a show try to remember that it is a sport and a hobby that you are pursuing. You should be able to win and also lose with good grace. It is a hard lesson to learn but there will be days at shows when you come lower down the line than you expected and inferior dogs to yours are put above you by the judge of the day. Remember that the interpretation of the breed standard is a personal opinion and one judge will prefer a different specimen to another. In time you will learn to know which judges admire the virtues which are strongest in your dogs and which admire other virtues and in this way you will be able to pick and choose under which judges you are prepared to enter.

It pays to have a sense of humour and a sporting nature if you are to pursue the fascinating and absorbing hobby of dog showing.

Many people will go to a show expecting to win and become extremely upset when they fail to win the prize they expected. This is transmitted to all the others around the ring and can totally spoil everyone else's day. You will soon become known for the way you conduct yourself in and out of the ring. So be prepared to smile and accept defeat gracefully and congratulate the person above you on that occasion no matter what your thoughts and feelings are, another day it will be your turn. If you cannot accept defeat without showing your disgust to everyone at the ringside it is better that you stay at home. For some people the desire to win is so great that it becomes an all consuming passion and anything less than Best of Breed is failure to them. Everyone wants to win who enters a dog show but you should enter for the fun and pleasure it gives you and for the company you meet at the show and not just the glory of winning.

Eng. and Irish Champion Candida of Crinan gained her English title in 1975 at Windsor Ch. Sh. She was shown by the handler Mr Geof. Corish. He had earlier that year shown her at Cruft's where she gained the Bitch Challenge Certificate.

The best way to start showing, if you think you have these attributes, is by attending a few shows as an observer. You will be able to find out the venues of the shows by consulting one of the weekly dog papers or alternatively, if it is a breed show that you want to attend, contact the secretary of the breed club and they will be able to give you details of any shows in the near future. You will find it most likely that you will have to travel a good distance to breed shows but you will certainly find a general show in your area. You may also be lucky and have a society devoted to the terrier breeds in general. Most local shows only have one or two terrier classes on the schedule. Go along to these shows and talk to the exhibitors but remember, if they are grooming their dogs prior to entering the ring they may have little time for casual conversation. You are more likely to get help and information if you approach them after they have finished showing their dogs. It is a good idea to try and get to know a few people before you go to your first show as an exhibitor as they will be able to give you help and advice if you should need it at a later date. As a beginner you may find it hard to know who to ask for advice. My advice to you is to go and make yourself known to the club secretary, he or she will then be able to steer you towards someone in the club who will be only too willing to offer help and advice and who has gained experience of the breed and dog showing over many years.

You may have a specimen of the breed which is very good but however excellent he is or however beautifully groomed, he will not win anything if his deportment and behaviour are not up to scratch. So before you enter shows contact your local canine society and find out if they run a ring-craft class. This trains you and your puppy for the show ring as opposed to

A group of exhibitors showing their 'class winners' at a Championship Show. From *l. to r.*: the author; Miss J Johnson (Wistmill); Miss S Cleland (Birkfell); Miss F M C Cook (Famecheck); Mrs R Armstrong (Justrite).

obedience training. Although you want your 'Westie' to be generally obedient and responsive to your commands, obedience classes are of no use to the show dog. At the ring-craft class, as well as learning to show, he will also learn to accept the many different types of dog that he may meet at a local or general show, without becoming upset or frightened by them.

There are several different levels of dog show but all must be run with a licence from the Kennel Club. There are terrier shows and races sometimes run by the local hunt which do not come under the jurisdiction of the Kennel Club. An aspiring show dog should not be taken to these shows. You should make sure if you intend entering a small local show that it is licensed by the Kennel Club. Entry at an unlicensed show could cause you difficulties in the future.

Before you enter a show you must be registered as the owner of the dog by the Kennel Club. So as soon as you receive the registration papers from the breeder, fill in the 'transfer of ownership' form on the reverse side of the registration form and return it to the Kennel Club with the relevant fee. It is wise to make a photocopy of this important document so that you have all the relevant details should it get lost anywhere. You are allowed to enter your dog for a show after you return this form to the Kennel Club provided that you mark your entry T.A.F. (transfer applied for). When you receive the documents back from the Club with the dog transferred into your name, you can drop the use of the initials.

The only type of show exempt from this ruling of registration is the Exemption Show. These are usually held in conjunction with local carnivals, flower shows or fêtes and are fun to attend as well as being good training for a young puppy. As well as this they are usually held to aid a local charity or other good cause which is an added reason for attending. Although the show is exempt from the fact that the dog being entered is registered at the Kennel Club, the show is still licensed by them.

Entry forms for these shows are usually a very simple affair and are filled in at the show venue just before judging is about to commence. The entry fee is usually very low when compared with the other types of show. Classes are usually of two types, 'pedigree' and 'fun' classes, the latter being open to mongrel as well as pedigree dogs. Here you will find the 'dogs with the waggiest tail' or the 'saddest expression'. Many of the classes are well filled with as many as forty exhibits and therefore the whole show must be thought of 'as a fun day out' for you and your dog and a good opportunity to get to know other dog owners in your locality.

Kennel Club shows are divided into four different types. Each one requires that you fill in an entry form and send it with the full entry fee to the secretary, to arrive before a 'closing date'. Each form requires to know

Mrs Mary Torbet showing
Ch. Glengordon Hannah.

the name of the dog, as registered at the Kennel Club, the date of birth,
owner, breeder and breed of dog, also the sire and dam. If you make an
incorrect declaration in any of these areas you can be liable for disqualifica-

tion, so always re-check entry forms. As well as these details you will have to state which classes you want to enter. At any but Championship shows there may be a wide choice available to you. They may include:

Age classes

Minor puppy	6 to 9 months
Puppy	6 to 12 months
Junior	6 to 18 months

Classes restricted by numbers of wins

Maiden, novice, tyro, limit, open etc.

Breed or group classes

West Highland White Terrier, Any variety (A.V.) Terrier, A.V. Sporting Terrier, A.V. Sporting, A.V. Scottish Native Breeds, A.V. Short Legged Terrier etc.

On the entry you will be asked to sign a declaration that the details are correct and that your dog has not recently suffered from or come into contact with any infection nor that he has suffered from any effect of inoculation.

 As you are signing a declaration that you will abide by Kennel Club

The Certificate or 'Ticket' given to the winner of Best Sex at a Championship Show.

This is later followed by the official certificate from the Kennel Club.

regulations, it would be a good thing to read through a copy to see to what regulations you have agreed to keep.

The types of show covered by the Kennel Club regulations come in four types and at no show can a puppy under six months of age be entered. These shows are:

Sanction shows: You will be required to join the club or society running the show and dogs that are multiple first prize winners at open and championship show level are barred from entry by the type of class scheduled.

Limited shows: These are also limited to members of the club or society, so on entering the show you will also have to pay a membership fee. This lasts for one year and will cover all the shows held in that year. The only dogs unable to enter are those dogs that have been awarded K.C. Challenge Certificates at Championship Shows.

Open Shows: These are open to all exhibits and can be all breeds or restricted to a group or a single breed. The West Highland White Terrier Club of England does hold a restricted open show in which the exhibition of champions is not allowed.

Championship Shows: These are the most important types of show, as well as being the most expensive to enter. They are open to all the breeds and varieties scheduled at that show, with Challenge Certificates on offer in the majority of breeds. At the present time all general Championship Shows schedule West Highland White Terriers and all have Challenge Certificates on offer. There are also Championship Shows run by the four Breed Clubs and an extra show (combined) run in turn by, at the present time, three of the Clubs. As well as these there are two group Championship Shows where you will be able to enter. These are the National Terrier Championship Show and the relatively new Scottish Breeds Championship Show.

There is also another qualification that has to be won at Championship Shows and that is entry to Crufts Championship Show. Only Champions and stud book holders are admitted by right, others having to qualify by winning a first in one of the specified classes in the year preceding Crufts. Each year it is necessary to re-qualify.

The most coveted award at these shows is the Challenge Certificate known by exhibitors as the C.C. or 'the ticket'. To win one of these the dog or bitch must be declared best of its sex at that show. It must also be worthy of the title of Champion because if the dog or bitch does not come up to the standard the judge believes necessary he can withhold the C.C. In this case he would merely award a Best of Sex certificate. The judge on the C.C. has to sign a declaration that he is clearly of the opinion that the chosen animal 'is of such outstanding merit as to be worthy of the title of Champion'.

To become a Champion a dog or bitch has to win three of these certificates under three different judges. One of these certificates must be won after the dog or bitch reaches its first birthday but apart from this there is no time limit and once the title is confirmed the West Highland keeps the title for ever.

Mention must also be made of another much sought after award, the 'Junior Warrant'. This is won when the dog is between six and eighteen months of age. Points can be gained only at Open and Championship level in breed competition. To gain the title of Junior Warrant it is necessary to amass 25 points. These can be gained by winning a first prize in an open show breed class which gives one point or a first prize in a breed class at a Championship Show for which three points are awarded. As you can see this means that a dog will have to be fairly consistent in his prize winning to gain the title in 12 months of showing. Only a handful of West Highlands are successful each year and although it does not make any difference to the title, some dogs have been known to get in excess of 75 points. The highest score of which I am aware was nearing the 100 mark, no mean achievement for dog and owner, as it involves a vast amount of travelling throughout the year.

To return to the Championship Show. You may never in many, many years of showing be fortunate enough to win a Challenge Certificate which should be the ultimate goal of all exhibitors but it is nice to aim for the top, not forgetting that once there it is harder to fall. It is quite a comedown to win the C.C. and even Best of Breed at one show only to go onto the next show and come out of the ring without any type of award.

The premier show of the year and one which is most talked about by the general public is Crufts. At one time it was just another Championship show run by Charles Cruft but after his death it was taken over and run by the Kennel Club. It is a show which to many exhibitors is the peak of the show calendar but even those who qualify will often shun the show because of the venue and the time of year which makes it a marathon in terms of endurance. Many exhibitors who attend say 'Never again' but many make the pilgrimage year after year. Perhaps it is the special atmosphere made by the trade stands, TV cameras and lights and overseas visitors that makes it so special for so many people. It is the aim of many exhibitors to win a C.C. at Crufts although this is no different to any other C.C. won during the year.

The highlight of the day's judging at Crufts is the Terrier Group and although several West Highlands have come close to winning this, only two have succeeded. They were Ch. Dianthus Buttons in 1976 who later that week went on to win the top honour of Supreme Best in Show, and Ch. Jaimont of Whitebriar in 1985.

Showing the West Highland White Terrier

Many West Highlands are natural showers and as much use of this should be made as possible. In the chapter on grooming, I suggested that your dog should be stood on a table for his daily grooming sessions. This grooming session should also be used to teach him manners on the table so that when he comes to his first show, the way he is handled will not be strange to him. Make him stand quietly on the table with his head held gently looking straight ahead, encourage him not to hold his nose in the air and do not 'string him up' so tightly on the lead that his pads hardly reach the ground. Check that the front legs are placed in the correct position, parallel to each other when viewed from the front, with a space between the legs. This will of course vary with the age and size of the dog but they should not be very close together. If any adjustment in placing should be necessary, do this very gently from the elbow, usually slight inward pressure will be sufficient to make the dog reposition his feet. Do not pick him up by the paws to re-adjust them as I have found that a West Highland does not like this form of interference and is more likely to place his feet even more awkwardly. Also it is likely to push in the hair around the pads and ankles, giving the appearance of a crooked front.

Next run your hands down the back of the neck and along the top line, this in time will allow him to realise that you are about to touch him behind the tail. A dog approached directly from behind is more likely to be surprised and move from the position in which you have stood him. Now make sure that his back legs are correctly placed. Viewed from the side, the hocks should be seen at right angles to the table surface. If pulled further out, the top line of the terrier will start to slope from shoulder to tail as seen in many gundogs. The hocks will also be placed into such a position that if he were on the floor it would be impossible for him to start to move forward before he repositioned his legs more naturally. Viewed from the rear his hocks should be parallel to each other. I have found the best way to place the dog in such a position if he does not naturally adopt it, is to use the left hand to ease his weight off the hind feet by putting your hand between his legs from behind and gently easing the weight off his legs and at the same time easing them forward. This should only be a slight adjustment. If the dog is not of the correct structure, either being cow-hocked or over long in the hock, it would be impossible to get him to stand correctly and hairdressing has to be employed in order to try and hide this fault from the judge who, if he is worth his salt, will find it anyway. Finish off the lesson in standing on the table by running your hand up the dog's tail from base to tip but don't push it too far over his back or this will make the tail set look wrong and you should encourage him to hold up his own tail. Before you put your dog on the floor get someone to approach the youngster as if he were the judge and check him over so that he is used to being examined by a stranger. The dog's lips should be drawn back to examine the teeth, both at the front and side. If you go to a ring-craft class this is the way in which you would stand your dog on the table when it comes for your turn to be judged.

On entering the show ring you should stand your dog in the same manner. If possible stand up to do this and, if he will do so, allow him to hold his own tail upright. If he is interested in the dog next to him or something else going on in or around the ring he may show himself off to better advantage, without any interference from you. Learn to judge when your dog is looking right. If a dog shows with as little interference from you as possible it cannot be anything but good. I have often seen dogs ruined by over-handling and this is not always by the novice handler.

Watch others from the ringside and see how they get the most out of their dogs. As long as your dog is standing reasonably still for the judge to see his good points it should not be necessary for him to stand like a stuffed toy, showing no animation for long periods of time. It's nice to see a West Highland staring hard at you as you walk down the line of dogs, almost daring you not to put him up. Something of the charm and character is all too often lost in an over-trained West Highland.

When asked to move your dog, move around the ring in an anti-clockwise direction, with your dog on your left, never coming between the dog and the judge. Move the dog on a loose lead, never string him up so that his feet barely touch the ground as this can destroy the correct forward movement. Walk at a speed best suited to the dog. Some move more slowly than others but none-the-less correctly. Do not be misled into thinking that because the handler of another dog is almost running his dog must be covering more ground with each stride, this is not necessarily true.

Next you will put your dog on the table for the judge before being asked by him to move your dog for individual inspection. The usual figure for movement is a triangle and if indoors, rubber mats are laid for the dog to move on, however outdoors you have to make your own triangle. Again keep your dog to your left, move away from the judge in a straight line, turn left at the bottom of the ring and go in a straight line to the opposite corner before turning left again and heading straight towards the judge. This allows him to assess movement from both front and rear as well as from the side. Be aware of where the judge is at all times because he may move to assess some other point of the dog whilst on the move. When you near the judge at the end of the triangle, alert the dog and try to make the most of his expression. The judge himself will often do this and then you may be asked to walk your dog again but listen carefully to the instructions of the judge and follow them as accurately as possible. After your dog has been seen by the judge, return to your place in the line behind the other dogs judged before you and allow your dog a little time to relax. When the judge starts to look at the last dog in the class, settle your dog and stand him again for as soon as the last dog has been examined, the judge will walk along the line to pick the winners of the class. This may be a quick decision or it may take some time. If the class is large the judge may pick out dogs for further consideration and ask the rest to leave the ring. If you are asked to do either of these do it as quickly as you can without upsetting your own or any other dog in the ring. You may be lucky and be placed or your day in the ring may be over, whichever happens accept the judge's decision with good grace, if possible congratulating those above you, on another occasion the tables will be turned. Remember the old saying 'do unto others as you would be done by'.

When the day for your first show arrives, allow plenty of time for the journey and for parking the car. At a general championship show you may well have quite a long walk from the car park to the hall or benching tent. A novice dog's whole show career can be spoilt by a late arrival and rushing into the ring at the last minute. You and your puppy will arrive in the ring without having had any time to compose yourselves.

Ch. Domaroy Erisort Seranade. A natural show lady owned by Mr and Mrs R Wilshaw.

Once the 'bug' has bitten and you learn to love and enjoy showing it is most likely that you will want to enlarge your family of West Highlands and your experience gained in the show ring will help you if you wish to make another purchase.

You may have to face the problem that your once good show dogs are now too elderly for the show ring and if you want to continue showing, you may need to rehouse your older dogs. West Highlands seem to settle well when this happens but great care should be taken when rehousing because not all proposed foster homes are as genuine as at first you may think. So that this does not occur I try to space my dogs so that a new youngster comes along every few years and I never have more dogs than I can comfortably take with me on any journey I may make. If, for any reason, it becomes necessary to find my dogs a new home bitches are always spayed and both dogs and bitches go to their new homes purely as companions. My most recent departure has been my much loved bitch Ch. Crinan Celtic Song. Britta, although only four years of age, had a difficult whelping and it was my vet's advice that she should not be bred from again. She settled quickly into her new home, enjoying life as a companion and her new owner later commented to me that her coming had given life more meaning. Never since the loss of her old dog had she spoken to so many people all wanting to know about her new friend.

Although it is hard to part with your dogs it is usually a good thing for both the dog and its new owner. Although the occasional one finds a new home, I find the process very difficult as do many other breeders who have their dogs as companions in the home. My oldest bitch who is still occasionally shown is now thirteen and is quite happy to teach the young puppies all her tricks. I think that a well balanced puppy is formed by mixing with the adults and sometimes being told off by great grandma.

If you have had a bitch which has done reasonably well in the show ring you may have decided that it would be a good idea to mate her in order to start your own line. Never consider mating a bitch merely to make money because you are doomed to failure. It should be your aim to breed an occasional litter when you would like to keep something from that bitch to show. It is interesting to scan through a show catalogue and note the exhibitor who has an almost constant stream of puppies from a certain bitch but sooner or later the bitch or puppies will suffer and this is not what the responsible dog breeder wants from his stock.

9 Breeding

A group of show dogs from the Lasara Kennels with their owners Miss Jane Kabel and Mrs Barbara Graham. *l to r*: Lasara Leman; Lasara Look-out (sister of Int. Ch. L. Look Here); Lasara Liza-Jane (dam of Ch. L. Lady Sue); Ch. Birkfell Sunbright (by Int. Ch. L. Lots of Fun); Ch. Lasara Like-a-Lot (by Int. Ch. L. Lots of Fun); Lasara Little Toss; Can. Ch. Haweswalton Man About Town (by Int. Ch. L. Lots of Fun) and Lasara Lianne.

If you are considering the possibility of breeding or starting your own kennel then you will have chosen a bitch or a stud dog as close to the breed standard as possible. Before you embark on a breeding programme you should consider your motives. Even the most experienced breeders have made mistakes in the past and it is sad to see West Highlands used for commercial gain in multi-breed establishments or ending up in the breed rescue because they have become a nuisance or the owners have bought a new 'toy'.

If you think that the money raised by the sale of a litter would be a useful addition to the family budget, you would do well to think again. The expenses involved, even before the arrival of the litter, can be great. Such

A group of show dogs from the Lasara Kennels with their owners Miss Jane Kabel and Mrs Barbara Graham. *l to r*: Lasara Leman; Lasara Look-out (sister of Int. Ch. L. Look Here); Lasara Liza-Jane (dam of Ch. L. Lady Sue); Ch. Birkfell Sunbright (by Int. Ch. L. Lots of Fun); Ch. Lasara Like-a-Lot (by Int. Ch. L. Lots of Fun); Lasara Little Toss; Can. Ch. Haweswalton Man About Town (by Int. Ch. L. Lots of Fun) and Lasara Lianne.

things as travel to the stud dog and the fee payable as well as possible vet's fees for checking the bitch, can soon mount up to more than the value of one puppy. As well as this you will need to have better quality food for the bitch. Certain items will be an expense with first-time litters but can be used for subsequent litters. They consist of whelping boxes, heating pads and special blankets for the box. These are a necessity so that the bitch can raise her expected litter in security and comfort. After the birth of the litter the expenses will continue with extra nourishing food for the dam, heating bills, vet's fees and later on the food for weaning and feeding the puppies. It is also your responsibility to register the litter of puppies with the Kennel Club.

This is, of course, if everything goes according to plan. You may also have the disappointment of a bitch who misses and therefore there would be no income for the initial outlay or the bitch may need a caesarean operation and there is a chance that she may have no live puppies or that you may lose your family pet. So you must consider very carefully whether the risk you are undertaking is really worthwhile.

There are many old wives' tales about bitches having litters and many are just that. It is often thought that to have a litter from a bitch that has frequent false pregnancies will put an end to them but this is not so. She may continue to have false pregnancies and the only way to stop them would be to have her spayed. A bitch with a history of false pregnancies can be sometimes difficult to get into whelp. It is also untrue that to have a litter from a bitch will stop her developing pyometra in later life. Even bitches who have had a litter can develop this. It is often thought to be good for a bitch to have 'just one litter'; this is not true as many bitches can go right through life perfectly healthy and happy without the necessity of having a litter. In fact some bitches detest puppies, going as far as killing them within a few hours of their birth.

First consider the disadvantages as well as the thought of having a litter and if in any doubt about whether you can cope, don't go any further. If, after thorough consideration about cost, morals and time involved over a period of about twelve weeks, you think everything is worth the risk involved, then go ahead. Before doing so it is probably advisable for the vet to give your bitch a thorough check to see that she has no physical abnormalities which would either make whelping difficult or be passed on to her puppies.

The stud dog

As the owner of a bitch it will be necessary to consider which stud dog you want to use well in advance of the mating. The dog may be in demand and

English and Canadian Ch.
Newtonglen Footprint
(dog).

it may not, therefore, be possible to fit in a bitch at the last minute. Contact the breeder of your bitch and ask her for advice on the choice of a stud dog. Most breeders will be only too pleased to advise which lines to choose from and which lines to avoid. Through many litters they will have gained experience invaluable to the novice. Failure to give assistance would only reflect on them ultimately, as if a poor litter is produced it would, no doubt, be blamed on the breeding. If, as a novice, you fail to get advice from others you have only yourself to blame if the outcome is disastrous.

When choosing a stud dog for your bitch there are other points that should also be considered as well as consulting the breeder. It is not a wise move to choose the top winning dog of the period or even the top stud dog because if the lines of that dog do not suit your bitch the outcome will not be successful. This may be something that the breeder of the bitch may be able to tell you. It may have been found from past litters that using a certain line would produce a very undesirable fault and this should be avoided if at all possible.

Assess your own bitch and beware of her faults, for to use a stud dog with the same faults would merely accentuate the fault. Study the breed in the show ring and mark in the catalogue any specimens that you like for their breed type, also for their strengths where your bitch is weak. Then go

Ch. Ashgate Achnasheen (dog).

home and study the catalogue as it is not those dogs themselves that you should be interested in but their sire and dam. Firstly note if the dam has breeding in common to your own, this will give you some idea of whether you could risk the use of the same sire. You may find that many different lines on the dam's side when mated to the same sire are giving the same uniform breed type. This means that the stud dog is very dominant. Some breeders of excellent bitch lines do not like to use a very dominant dog as it has a tendency to change the type of bitch they have produced over many generations. Certain dogs are known for their ability to produce a particularly good point with a fair amount of consistency in whichever bitch is mated to them. Although it can be the boast of many stud dog owners that their dog is siring particularly fine puppies, the reply of the owner of the bitch must be 'but how are the bitches bred' for each is of importance when planning a litter of puppies.

It may be difficult to assess the merits of certain stud dogs if few of their offspring are in the ring, nevertheless this does not make them any the less important for the use they may be to you in a breeding programme. There are many dogs who appear regularly as sires who have themselves, for one reason or another, made little or no impact in the show ring but their progeny are well to the fore in show results. A popular stud dog may produce a hundred puppies in many litters and have twenty of them winning in the ring. A less popular dog may have almost as many winning stock from a much smaller number of puppies born. With a little research this is something that can, if time is available, be checked in the Kennel Club Stud Record Book.

Your duty is to produce as good a litter as possible by using the correct dog for your bitch. It costs little or nothing more to produce quality puppies of which anyone would be proud, even if most of them are to be sold as pets and only the best one retained by you for show purposes.

Many kennels nowadays are run on a small scale, keeping only one dog and a few bitches which all live in the house as companions. If this is going to be the case with you it is important for the management of the dogs that you have adequate space to be able to separate the dog from the bitches when any of them are in season. To have a stud dog for use on your own bitches is not usually a good idea. If the dog is one bred by yourself it will very likely be too close to your own bitches' breeding to be of use to them. Also, if this is not the case, you may find after one litter that the combination of the two results in a rather mediocre litter. This can happen even if both are champions.

A stud dog should be separated from bitches in season and if possible allowed a totally different exercise area. A dog, if a keen stud, will lose a lot of weight and condition in a very short time if he is subjected to the constant smell of bitches in season. It may even put him off his job as a stud dog, as when he is expected to mate a visiting bitch he may not be as receptive to the smell of a bitch in season as he would normally be.

The young dog: Although it should be fairly natural for a dog to mate a bitch, there is a certain amount of training and familiarization that should go hand in hand with his early life as a dog and his work as a stud dog. A young male puppy will quite frequently mount other puppies in the litter of both sexes and to push him off or chastise him, will start to build up in his mind doubts about mounting a bitch. If this prohibition is repeated frequently it could, in later life, lead to a complete refusal by the dog to mate a bitch and at the approach of the owner to help the mating he would merely jump off and run away from the bitch. The behaviour of the youngster has to be tolerated, taking care that in his exuberance he does not start a fight, as his kennel mates of either sex may not like his advances. Occasional praise is in order, as is going over to him and stroking him and this will get him used to the idea of being helped when later on he is ready to mate his first bitch.

A dog can be first used at stud when he is around ten months of age but do not be in a hurry to use him, wait until the right bitch comes along. You may find that she is nothing special as far as looks are concerned but it is more important that she has a steady temperament and is willing to stand patiently for the inexperienced dog. It is preferable for the bitch to have had a litter before, as the reason for using your dog at stud the first time is to 'prove him'. This means to show bitch owners that he is capable of siring a litter of puppies. If for no fault of his own the dog mates several bitches and fails to produce a litter, the word soon spreads and the days of his stud career could turn out to be very brief.

Cedarfell Masterfull (dog) grandson of Ch. Cedarfell Merry-n-Bright.

It is usual to use some form of restraint when mating a dog to a bitch and this can vary according to the owner of the dog's requirements but it is up to the bitch owner to accept this. Sometimes the bitch is required to be muzzled or a tape tied round her muzzle to prevent her snapping. Even an even-tempered bitch can put up a surprising show of aggression to the consternation of the owners. Another practice is to hold the bitch by a loose-fitting collar to stop her fighting. Mating can take place either on a table or on the floor. An experienced stud dog will not care where the bitch is as long as she seems ready for mating. The young dog, however, may need some encouragement and patience may be needed, also a little help before he eventually succeeds in mating the bitch.

Initially it may be of help to the young dog to 'flirt' with the bitch for a few minutes and arouse his interest. After a short time kneel down in front of the bitch if she is on the floor or sit if she is to be mated on a table and hold the bitch firmly but kindly by the collar, remembering that she also may need reassurance. Mating requires two pairs of hands and a first mating should have as an assistant, someone who is used to holding a bitch although this may not be possible and the owner of the bitch may have to assist. If he or she is a novice owner, time should be taken to explain exactly what you want them to do.

Some dogs need little or no assistance in mating a bitch and all that is necessary is a hand behind the tail of the dog to prevent him from losing his balance. However, some bitches may prove more difficult to mate and resent the attentions of the male and it is for this reason that you should accustom the stud dog to accept any help that may be required. The bitch may have to be held in a standing position whilst the dog is being supported in the rear. He may, because of the over-large size of the bitch, have to be raised slightly higher off the ground than the bitch – I don't know what British Telecom would think about this use of the Yellow Pages! All these things should become acceptable to the dog in a matter of time but may put a young dog off if not properly handled.

After the young dog has been used for the first time at stud, it is wise to wait some time before using him on another bitch. My usual procedure is to wait and see if the first bitch has a litter before I will use him again at stud. A dog that is used too much when young may very soon lose the urge to mate bitches so it is very important to manage a dog carefully to ensure that this does not happen. If he has been used at stud and proved that he can sire a litter, a stud fee can be charged. For the first mating, however, no stud fee should be charged until the bitch proves to be in whelp or produces a litter. If it is your bitch that is mated to a maiden dog, you should not, however, expect to receive any papers until the relevant stud fee has been paid in a way specified by the owner of the stud dog.

Each owner of a stud dog should keep a receipt book with the names and details of all bitches served by the dog, along with the owner's name, address and 'phone number. You should also note on both sections, any details particular to that mating. Some will be for your own use but some will be to prevent a misunderstanding occurring at a later date between you and the owner of the bitch. For your information, you could note the sire and dam of the bitch and also whether the mating was very good, the length of tie etc or whether the bitch proved difficult to mate. For the bitch owner, it may be wise to note whether or not she will be allowed a free service should she not take.

After a stud dog has sired a litter it is the practice to pay a stud fee in full after a successful mating. The fee is for that mating and not for any puppies that may be expected. Most owners of stud dogs will allow that same bitch to return for another mating the next time she is in season if she should fail to conceive on the first occasion. This should be checked with the owner of the dog at the time of mating as it cannot be considered your right to demand this service. If the stud dog is very popular or is sold abroad, you may not be able to return to the same dog. For the same reason a bitch may only be able to have one mating. If the dog has proved to be very fertile, multiple matings at one season should not be necessary.

If a free mating is to be taken up for the next season, it is only good manners to inform the owner of the stud dog that your bitch has not had puppies. This should be done as near as possible to the date she was due to whelp. You will receive no sympathy at all if you wait until the bitch is in season again before informing the stud dog owner.

It is for this reason that I personally do not give the Kennel Club blue form to the owner of the bitch after mating. In this way the owner must ring or write to me notifying me of the outcome of the mating and it enables me to keep an exact tally of what my stud dog is siring. The blue form must be signed by the owner of the dog, stating when the bitch was mated and the full particulars of the dog used. Without this form, the owner of the bitch would be unable to register the litter with the Kennel Club. It is easier, as the owner of a stud dog, for you to hold a stock of these forms so that there is no delay in getting them to the bitch owner as soon as one is requested. Remember to transfer details of the litter into your stud receipt book so that it can be referred back to should the need arise.

A dog used regularly at stud should be well fed and the quality of his food must be as good as that of a bitch in whelp, for if he is expected to mate a number of bitches he will be under some body stress and food of good quality should be given to counter-balance this. Many owners believe in the addition of Vitamin E to the diet.

One of the most difficult things you may have to do as the owner of a stud dog is to say 'no'. If you have the future of the breed at heart, times may arise when this is necessary. It may be for any number of reasons, you may know that the lines don't mix or you may not approve of the motives of the owner of the bitch for wanting a litter. However difficult it may be it is good that, as the owner of a stud dog, you have principles that you stick to come what may.

The bitch

The bitch will normally come into season somewhere between the ages of six and twelve months, although some can come into season much later

Ch. Crinan Candee J. W. (bitch). Not a champion until she was five years old. Some West Highlands mature at a very early age, but some as the one above are late maturers. They can continue their show career for many years, going into veteran at 7 years of age.

but this would be unusual and if the bitch has not had a season by the time she is fourteen months old it may be wise for a vet to check her over. It would be very unusual to mate a bitch the first time she is in season and she would usually be far too immature both in mind and body to cope with the extra strain put on her to rear a litter of puppies. It is far better to wait until her second or even third season before attempting to have a litter from her.

The first season is a very useful time to check the pattern of your bitch's season. Make a note of the date on which she first shows colour and how long this lasts before coming more clear. At the same time the vulva will start to swell and the muscles around it start to relax. This would normally happen at about twelve to fourteen days, although many bitches can show a different pattern. It is not at all unusual for most colour to have disappeared from the vaginal discharge by about the eighth or ninth day along with the other external signs. A season can also last much longer. If you intend to mate your bitch when a little older this is all very useful information which the owner of the stud dog will find helpful in assessing on which day your bitch should come to be mated to the dog. It is only when the bitch is ready for mating during this period that she will stand for the dog and allow herself to be mated. In some bitches that period of time during which she will stand may be several days and in others it may be as

Ch. Sumar Sosues owned and bred by Miss S. Jackson. Her sire was Ch. Checkbar Finlay MacDougal and dam Ch. Sumar Glengyle Tucket.

short as several hours. This second type may be very difficult to mate because of her unwillingness to stand quietly to be mated. The normal day for a bitch to be mated would be between the twelfth and fourteenth day of her season but if it was observed from the earlier season that she became 'flighty' at an earlier day, it would be as well to make arrangements to take her to visit the dog earlier than the twelfth day. Alternatively you may have noticed that the colour lasted longer and therefore the bitch should be mated later. I have known bitches at both extremes, one being mated on her fourth day, the other on the twenty-first day, both bitches having litters to these matings.

A normal season would be heralded by a hardening of the areas around the vagina with some swelling. This is a stage which in some bitches can be very noticeable whilst in others it is hardly visible at all. The length of this period can vary from a few days to a week or more. It is followed by more swelling and a bloody discharge which finally becomes pure blood. The amount of blood is very varied from bitch to bitch and sometimes very little will be noticed because the bitch will constantly clean herself. This stage will usually last about a week and after this the discharge becomes less copious and clearer and the vulva begins to soften, the softening being the warning that the time for mating is approaching. In the third week the swelling decreases and the discharge ceases by the end of this week, the organs having returned to normal.

If all this can be observed in the first 'heat' you will find the problem of knowing on which day to mate your bitch much decreased.

The interval between seasons can also vary but normal could be considered to be six months. The pattern of bitches can vary from four-and-a-half months upwards, seven months not being at all unusual. This should not cause any difficulty when the bitch comes to having a litter.

For the novice owner of a bitch, it is well to be aware of the length of a bitch's cycle because to be unaware of the fact that the season is happening would cause you problems. It is wise, during this three week period, to keep your bitch in her home territory. If it is necessary to take her out, carry her for a short distance away from home before putting her down to walk. This process should be repeated on the homeward journey. It is also helpful, if the bitch is not to be mated, to wash her down with 'Amplexol liquid'. This tends to kill the odour of the bitch and make it less likely that she will be followed. The effect of washing the bitch down can also be strengthened by giving her several 'Amplex tablets' a day. Other proprietary brands are available at your pet shop but their own perfume is rather powerful which you may find undesirable. You must realise that during this period your bitch may be very keen on the attentions of dogs in general, not confining herself to mere West Highlands. You may find local dogs which are allowed freedom to roam becoming a persistent nuisance. Dogs can, if necessary, jump what would otherwise appear to be insurmountable heights or tunnel under fences to reach their goal. It is also more than likely that your bitch could do the same thing.

Should the impossible happen there are two courses open to you, either take the bitch to the vet and he will give an injection which will make the season continue for a further three weeks or allow nature to take its course, even if the bitch has been mated to a dog of another breed. This will not influence in any way the ability of your bitch to produce a pure bred litter at a later date when mated to a West Highland. It was once believed that the influence of a previous sire could influence the offspring of a bitch by a subsequent and different sire (telegony). This was a view widely held in the nineteenth century but which is now a totally discredited theory due to more accurate observations and knowledge of heredity. It is sometimes even believed by some breeders of today but there is no truth in it.

There are of course two other ways of preventing an unwanted pregnancy but if you are taking either of these actions I would have thought that it would have been better for you to have a male in the first place than to have the worry of a season every six months or so.

The first way to prevent the bitch coming into season or to delay a season is by the use of contraceptive preparations available from your vet. They come in tablet form or injections. These are preparations of hormones and the instructions issued by the vet for their use should be followed carefully. I would not myself use this preparation, especially if it was contemplated breeding from the bitch at a later stage.

The other method would be to spay the bitch, thus preventing all possibility of her having a litter. If this is an absolute necessity care should be taken as to the timing of the operation. Never spay a bitch before her first season as to do so would be to stop her reaching full maturity. You would be increasing the risk of her developing certain bladder conditions and also dermatitis of the vulva which is difficult to treat. It is not unknown for a spayed bitch to lose her personality and it is also said that she will put on weight and become grossly overweight although if the food intake is correctly regulated this should not be allowed to happen. The disadvantages of spaying could possibly become more of a nuisance than allowing a bitch to come into season naturally and taking thorough care of her during this short period of time.

There are times when spaying may be used to stop considerable misery for the bitch. This is when she suffers constant and severe false pregnancies. This can occur either when the bitch has been mated or not. At the appropriate time after her season the bitch will show all the signs of being in whelp and it can be very difficult to tell the difference between a true and a false pregnancy. The condition can continue for varying lengths of time – some bitches recovering when the time for whelping has passed; others develop milk and become very broody, sometimes collecting their toys to look after or maybe someone's socks or sheepskin mittens. It is not unusual for this to continue past this period, the bitch regurgitating part of her digested food for the imaginary litter. This behaviour can become very distressing and should receive some sort of treatment from your vet.

When the time comes that you are ready to have a litter from your bitch and she is mature and healthy, watch her carefully for the signs that you have observed previously signalling the onset of her season. During the period that you are waiting for her to come into season, she should be treated for worms. Any worm eggs present in the bitch can infect the puppies before birth and for this reason she should be as free from eggs as possible.

At the first signs of any colour, inform the owner of the stud dog that you have previously chosen, that your bitch will soon be ready for mating. Do not expect to be fitted in at the last minute. Make a date and time when it is convenient for the owner of the dog and when you yourself can accompany the bitch to the stud dog. Watch your bitch carefully from now on for her normal pattern of season may not always happen. The day before you take the bitch to be mated 'phone and confirm your appointment for the next day. Arrive on time, for the owner of the stud dog may have had to disrupt her routine and nothing is more frustrating than waiting for someone to arrive. If you, for any reason at all, change your mind and decide not to mate the bitch, please inform the owner of the dog, she would probably also be interested in why you have changed your mind; it is better to withdraw at this stage than to have a litter of unwanted puppies with which you are unable to cope.

After your bitch has been served by the dog, allow her to rest quietly for a few hours if possible, before your return journey. If she is used to being in a box or crate this is a good place for her to go.

Ch. Birkfell Sunbright; bred by Miss S Cleland by English, Dutch and International Ch. Lasara Lots of Fun ex Birkfell So Simple, Owners Mrs B Graham and Miss J Kabel.

10 Pregnancy

After your bitch has been mated, take her home and treat her as normally as possible, sticking to the normal diet to begin with and keeping to the usual pattern of exercise.

To begin with there will be little noticeable change in the bitch but a very observant owner may well notice a change in temperament. Some bitches become quieter and more affectionate, whilst still remaining active. A bitch that becomes fat and lethargic in the early stages of pregnancy is more likely to be having a false pregnancy. Whilst it is normal for the appetite to increase some bitches can suffer from anorexia in the middle part of the pregnancy but this does not seem to have any marked effect on her puppies. Another change in mid pregnancy is the possible increase in her desire for water. Probably the most noticeable change in a bitch in whelp for the first time, is the enlargement and reddening of the teats, this becoming noticeable at about twenty-eight days. It is also at this time that your vet will be able to examine the bitch and tell you if she is in whelp. If left much longer than this the foetal units become surrounded in fluid and this combined with other changes in the bitch makes it almost impossible to feel the pea-shaped forms in the uterus. In any case it is very difficult to be able to say with any certainty how many puppies the bitch will have. Any other forms of test for positive pregnancy in a bitch are rather unreliable. At about twenty-eight days the individual foetal units measure about the size of a pea. These gradually grow and at about the forty-second day of pregnancy the uterine horns have to fold to allow for further development. It is at this time that an owner will have seen the bitch getting plumper and she suddenly appears to change shape. Instead of the bulges being on her side she starts to sag noticeably underneath. Also during this period, from about the thirty-second day, she will have a sticky discharge from the vulva. This may hardly be noticeable or it may be profuse and it becomes necessary to wash the bitch quite frequently. Without this discharge a bitch is unlikely to be in whelp. If the discharge does not begin until the later part of the pregnancy, between forty-two and forty-nine days, it is more likely to be the end of a false pregnancy.

During the final week of pregnancy the puppies can be felt moving and if she is having a large litter you may be able to see their feet kicking on the bitch's tummy. You can certainly feel this, as though there are little 'flicks' against the inside wall of the tummy.

The danger with many novice owners of a West Highland is that they may overfeed their bitch making her fat and not in a fit condition with good muscle tone to make her ready for whelping. During the first four weeks of pregnancy they need no extra food but from the fifth week the amount of food can be gradually increased. If you are feeding meat and biscuit increase the quality of meat, you may use eggs and fish as useful extras, also make sure that your bitch is receiving the correct amount of vitamins and minerals, the manufacturer's instructions should be followed with care.

By six weeks, the bitch may find it uncomfortable to eat all her food in one sitting. It is, therefore, wise to feed two meals a day of smaller quantity. If she will drink milk add this to her diet as it is an important source of extra calcium.

During the final few days of pregnancy, the bitch may not feed well, tending rather to pick at her food. Do not worry unduly about this as the time you really want a bitch to eat well is after the delivery of the puppies when the speed at which they put on weight can put a great demand on the bitch.

Whelping box

During the waiting period, you as the owner should not be idle. The whelping area must be prepared with a suitable bed and heat source long before the puppies are due, to enable the bitch to accustom herself to new sleeping quarters. Do not expect to put a bitch into the box when the birth is imminent, she will probably refuse to stay there and the disturbance could well delay the smooth whelping process.

The box itself can be bought or built by you and should be made of good quality wood which has been smoothed thoroughly. Cracks and holes in timber could well form a home for infection. For a West Highland the box itself should measure about 30 inches by 24 inches (75cm by 61cm) or a little larger. The construction of the box is a matter for personal preference but should be fitted with a top lid so that the puppies can be inspected more easily and more ventilation given if necessary. Some bitches prefer to have the lid open, others prefer a closed top. There should be a gate at the front. It is easier to manage if this is in two pieces, hinged from either side of the front. Around the inside of the box at about a height of 2 inches

(5cm) can be fitted a removable rail. This forms a 'crush bar' should a new-born puppy accidentally get between the bitch and the box itself. This only needs to stay in position for a week or two as very soon the puppy will be strong enough to pull itself from most tight spaces it may get into.

For the first few weeks of life the newly born puppies may require an extra heat source. It used to be provided by hanging an infra-red heater over the whelping box but this idea is now rather frowned upon. The heat provided was so severe that the bitch became unsettled and she herself would move out of the box. The most important and natural source of heat is the mother herself. The puppies will snuggle against her and keep warm and anything which disturbs this natural mothering habit should be discouraged.

Sometimes extra heat is necessary and this is best provided by a metal heated pad, specially made for the purpose. The modern variety is plugged into a transformer to step down the mains current to 12 volts. This is a useful safety feature, as the bitch may possibly dig up a mains cable and damage it, thus putting herself at risk. The metal pad can be placed to one side of the box so that the bitch can place herself away from it without having to leave the puppies. If possible place the cable of the pad so that it is inaccessible to the bitch. The pad should be placed underneath a thick layer of newspapers and on top of the newspapers place one of the new synthetic fur rugs, specially made for pet use. These are rather expensive but are worth the money for the extra comfort they give the bitch and her puppies. The other advantages are that any urine made by the puppies and not cleaned up by the bitch will pass straight through onto the papers beneath. They can also be boiled to reduce any risk of infection. At a later date when the puppies are starting to move around the fur provides a good foothold and encourages good movement, there being no danger of their small legs constantly slipping from under them as happens when they are reared on newspaper. The box and pad are quite expensive items but are things that can be used over many years. I prefer to use new 'fur' rugs for each litter that is born, using the others for the older dogs in their own beds and in their travelling boxes.

When you have made the whelping box, put it in a quiet place away from the attentions of the rest of the kennel, where you expect the bitch to whelp. I prefer to whelp the bitch in a spare bedroom as she invariably chooses to have her puppies at dead of night and it is easier to keep a constant, but unobtrusive, watch on her from the spare bed rather than constantly walking in and out of another room or even having to go outside to a whelping kennel. A bitch in the process of whelping should be close at hand at all times. It would be inhuman and a great risk to dam and litter to be left by themselves. I have heard that some people get away with it but I am not prepared to put my bitches at this risk.

Normal whelping

The normal gestation period for a bitch is sixty-three days, but it is not by any means unusual for a bitch to whelp several days early. A bitch can also whelp late but it is very unwise to let a bitch go over the period of sixty-three days without consulting your vet for there are reasons why the bitch may be late and which could necessitate the vet's intervention. Puppies born on the fifty-sixth day onwards are viable but earlier than this and it would be likely that the litter is at considerable risk. It is a wise precaution to have notified the vet about the date that your bitch is due to whelp. Make absolutely sure that either he or a locum will be available at any time, night or day, should you require assistance. Remember, if in any doubt at all you should call for assistance, it is false economy to adopt a 'wait and see' policy.

It is well to have various things to hand when the bitch is due to whelp. These are:

1. Some old towels cut up into squares of about 18 inches (45cm). These will assist you to hold onto the whelp should the bitch require manual assistance and also to rub the pups in the process of resuscitation.

2. Clean newspapers.

3. Cardboard box with a warm water bottle and some soft bedding.

4. A small amount of whisky, useful for helping to bring round an apparently lifeless puppy (a touch on the end of the tongue is all that is necessary).

FIG 28 A normal whelping

Puppy just about to be delivered.

Puppy delivered with afterbirth. If the bitch makes no move to remove the puppy from the bag, action should be taken immediately.

Also have at the ready milk or water with glucose and honey for the bitch to drink if required during the long whelping.

The whelping process can be divided into three stages:

1. The relaxation and dilation of the cervix.
2. The cervix is fully dilated and the foetus moves down and engages with the pelvic bone.
3. The expulsion of the puppies each in their own membrane and the expulsion of the placenta.

The first stage: This is very variable from none being observed at all to as long as forty-eight hours. It is unlikely that no first stage exists but sometimes the bitch will have carried on so normally with the routine that no changes will have been noticed. At the other end of the range, the longer time may be considered as abnormal. Between six and twenty hours is most usual.

The most reliable guide to the onset of whelping is the marked drop in the temperature of the bitch. The temperature of a bitch during the last few weeks of pregnancy is already low – 100°F – but in most cases the temperature goes down to between 97° and 99°F. It may stay at this level for only a few hours so it is necessary to repeat the process at intervals. The first stage of labour should commence within twenty-four hours of the low-point in the temperature.

Other points that are seen during the first stage of labour are: nest making in the newspaper of the whelping box, increased frequency of the need to urinate, and shivering. All the above symptoms will become more noticeable as the first stage progresses. Failure to do so should put you on the alert.

The second and third stages: The second stage is usually said to begin when the bitch's manner changes and she starts to strain to expel the puppies. Some bitches seem to make little effort to strain, then give one hard push and the puppy is born. Others seem to have to make much greater effort to give birth, the straining becoming more regular and frequent as the puppy nears the point of being expelled.

This period can cause the greatest concern to a novice as it is hard to decide when the bitch is progressing normally and when something is amiss. It is wise to inform the vet if no puppy has arrived two hours after the onset of straining. He will then advise on a course of action.

The first puppy may be preceded by a water bag. This can easily be mistaken for a puppy but is in fact a skin or membrane containing a greenish-black fluid. The size and shape of the water bag can vary with the

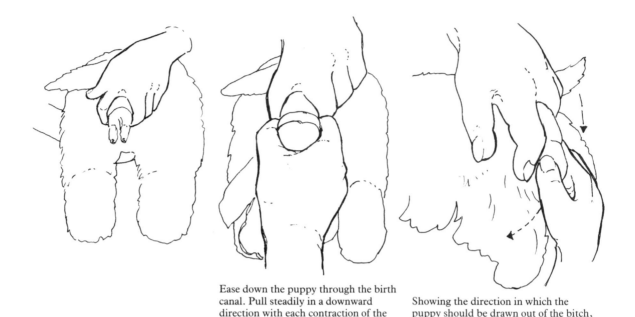

Ease down the puppy through the birth canal. Pull steadily in a downward direction with each contraction of the bitch.

Showing the direction in which the puppy should be drawn out of the bitch, between the hind legs.

FIG 29 The position of hands when assisting the bitch.

length of time the bitch has taken to pass it. It may even burst before it is delivered causing the release of the fluid which will drain out of the bitch and be absorbed by the layers of newspapers in the whelping box.

The first puppy will normally arrive within one hour of the onset of meaningful straining and often appears much sooner. After the birth of the first puppy the bitch usually takes a quick rest before the straining begins again for the next puppy.

It is essential to be with the bitch throughout the second and third stages. First-time mothers may need help with a new-born puppy. Should the bitch not appear to know what to do when the puppy is born, rapid help is needed. Break the bag under the chin of the puppy using only your finger nails, this can be surprisingly tough. Remove the membrane from the mouth and nose of the puppy and normally a puppy will start to breathe straight away after this is removed. If this is not the case then massage the puppy firmly with a rough towel; rubbing the opposite way to the growth of hair seems to be particularly stimulating as this imitates the bitch's method of licking the puppy. If necessary administer a small drop of whisky to the tongue. This is usually sufficient to make the puppy draw in a sharp breath and then continue to breathe normally. A considerable period of time may elapse before the puppy starts to breathe but don't give up too easily. It may also be necessary to sever the umbilical cord. This should also be done with the finger nails. There is a large blood vessel which runs down the cord and to cut it with sharp scissors may cause bleeding. Instead milk the blood out of the vein and tear the cord working towards the puppy and leaving about 1 inch (2.5cm) of cord. Do not pull away from the puppy as you may cause damage in the form of an umbilical hernia.

Although it is normal for a puppy to arrive head first, it is by no means unusual for the puppy to arrive hind feet first and this should not be considered to be abnormal. You may find that some help is required by the bitch to expel the puppy and it is important to get the puppy out and breathing without too much delay but without undue stress to either bitch or puppy. Use a small piece of towel to hold the puppy firmly but not too tightly. As the bitch strains, gently pull the puppy in a downwards direction through the bitch's hind legs. This would be the normal direction the puppy would follow had it been born naturally. Some puppies arrive tail first and this can prove a little more difficult. Ease out the hind legs and the hips before following the course of action for a puppy born backwards. In these sorts of situation there is little time to call a vet as the puppy must be removed relatively quickly in order that it may live and to allow further puppies to be born. If she is allowed to strain for a considerable period of time getting nowhere, she will rapidly become exhausted and the lives of further puppies may be in danger.

During the birth of further puppies the earlier arrivals may be in danger of the bitch trampling on them and it is wise to have a small cardboard box with a hot water bottle and blanket at the ready. If necessary you can transfer the early arrivals to this box whilst the bitch carries on the whelping. Care must be taken because the bitch may resent this interference and you may simply have to move the puppies to the other side of the box onto the heated pad which has been placed under a blanket.

After the bitch has finished whelping, she should be allowed to rest quietly, after giving her a warm drink. For the first twenty-four hours after whelping the bitch should be kept on a light diet, fish and white meat are excellent and she should be offered several small meals a day along with plenty to drink.

Although many people, if the whelping is normal and there is the correct ratio of afterbirths to puppies, do not bother to have a veterinary inspection, I think it is a good idea to have the bitch and her puppies checked over soon after the whelping is complete. The vet will check to make sure that no puppies or afterbirths have been retained by the bitch and that her uterus has started to contract. If he thinks it necessary to give the bitch an antibiotic, ask also for a vitamin B injection. This will help to return the body to its normal balance, disturbed by the antibiotics. A check will also be made on each of the puppies for hind dew-claws as well as any other obvious abnormality such as cleft palate. If you decide to have the dew-claws removed this should be done before the age of five days. Although it is not essential to do so many breeders feel that to leave the dew-claws on a show dog destroys the line of the front legs. The main reason for removal should not be cosmetic. The dew-claws, however, can cause some trouble as they can get caught in clothing or if not attended to regularly, they may grow long and become impacted in the pad and cause the dog some pain.

A form is supplied by the Kennel Club for the registration of puppies. This has to be completed by the owner of the stud dog as well as the breeder of the litter.

The bitch, after whelping is complete, should be cleaned up using warm water as she can become quite badly stained after whelping unless she is cleaned up frequently. During the first week or two there is likely to be a good deal of discharge which will gradually decrease. When it becomes exposed to the air, the discharge becomes greenish and this must be

---

KENNEL CLUB APPLICATION FOR LITTER RECORDING & PUPPY REGISTRATION (FORM 1) PLEASE READ THE NOTES OVERLEAF BEFORE COMPLETING THE FORM.

LITTER RECORDING

NAME & ADDRESS OF BREEDER(S) (OWNERS OF DAM) See Note 1
SURNAME / INITIALS / MR/MRS/MISS/MS
ADDRESS
POST CODE / TELEPHONE

DECLARATION TO BE SIGNED BY BREEDER(S) See Note 3
I/We the breeder(s) of the litter certify the particulars are true to the best of my/our knowledge and belief. I/We further certify that the litter was born in the United Kingdom and that the dogs in the litter have not been registered previously with the Kennel Club or any recognised body. I/We also certify that the sire and dam are registered in the Register of the Kennel Club and recorded as owned by those shown on this form and agree to be bound by and submit to Kennel Club Rules and Regulations as the same may be amended from time to time.
DATE / SIGNATURE(S)

REGISTERED NAME OF DAM OF LITTER (Block Capitals) See Note 5

K.C. REGISTRATION NO. See Note 6

NAME & ADDRESS OF OWNER(S) OF SIRE See Note 2 / LITTER NO.
SURNAME / INITIALS / MR/MRS/MISS/MS
ADDRESS
POST CODE

CONFIRMATION OF MATING TO BE SIGNED BY OWNER(S) OF SIRE See Note 4
I/We hereby certify that the Dam named as identified to me/us was mated to the Sire on the date indicated and that the Sire was recorded as owned by me/us on that date. I/We also certify that the Sire is registered in the Register of the Kennel Club. I/We have read the instructions for completion of this form and agree to be bound by and submit to Kennel Club Rules and Regulations as the same may be amended from time to time.
DATE / SIGNATURE(S)

REGISTERED NAME OF SIRE OF LITTER (Block Capitals) See Note 5

K.C. REGISTRATION NO. See Note 6

BREED See Note 7		BREEDERS AFFIX (IF ANY) See Note 8	DATE OF BIRTH (See Note 9)	DATE OF MATING (See Note 9)	NO. OF PUPPIES IN LITTER See Note 10	
					DOGS	BITCHES

PUPPY REGISTRATION

	DOG or BITCH	COLOUR	K.C. USE	PREFERRED NAME	ALTERNATIVE NAME See Note 13	ENDORSEMENTS (IF ANY) See Note 15
1						
2						
3						
4						
5						
6						
7						
8						
9						
10						

OPTIONS

IF THE ABOVE NAMES ARE NOT AVAILABLE, THE KENNEL CLUB WILL SELECT NAMES UNLESS YOU INITIAL THIS BOX (See Note 14) ☐
PLEASE TICK IF YOU REQUIRE 3 GENERATION PEDIGREES (See Note 16) ☐
PLEASE TICK IF YOU REQUIRE THE BREED RECORDS SUPPLEMENT (See Note 17) ☐
PLEASE TICK IF YOU REQUIRE A VAT INVOICE (See Note 23) ☐

FEES
£5 PER LITTER
plus
£5 FOR EACH REGISTERED (Named) PUPPY
and
£1 FOR EACH UNREGISTERED (Un-named) PUPPY

FOR KENNEL CLUB USE ONLY

PLEASE DOUBLE CHECK THAT THE APPLICATION HAS BEEN SIGNED BY (a) THE BREEDER(S) and (b) THE OWNER(S) OF THE SIRE

washed from behind the bitch's tail and the backs of her legs to prevent any discoloration.

After whelping a bitch will be very loath to leave her litter even to relieve herself and it is necessary for a few days to coax her, you may even need to carry her out but this period soon passes and she will again be back to normal.

Apart from the initial inspection of the puppies, they should be handled as little as possible during the first two weeks of life although it can be very useful to weigh each puppy regularly. This can give a good idea of each puppy's progress and can give an early warning that all is not well with an individual member of the litter. It is very difficult to spot that one puppy is not putting on the weight it should whilst others are gaining normally. Only when it becomes obviously smaller will you suddenly realise that something is wrong and this may be too late to take action. It may only be that one puppy is slightly smaller than its litter mates at birth and tends to get pushed away from the more productive teats thus the slight difference

'Family Group'. Mother, Grandmother, Daughter. They are owned by Mr and Mrs T W Johnson (Snojo).

at birth would become magnified as the days pass. The small puppy could then be helped to get a better share of the milk and the shortfall in weight could be regained.

In the first week a puppy will normally double its birth weight and this process will continue for several weeks, so any failure to put on weight may signify that something is wrong. Check that the bitch has enough milk for the amount of puppies she is feeding, it may be necessary to supplement her milk with a special milk powder made for hand-rearing puppies. It is interesting to note the weight gain in a litter of puppies born by caesarean section, over a period of three weeks.

DAY	1	2	3	4	5	6	7	8	9	10	11	12
DOG	$7\frac{1}{2}$	7	7	7	$7\frac{1}{2}$	8	$8\frac{1}{2}$	$10\frac{1}{2}$	12	13	14	15
BITCH 1	$7\frac{1}{2}$	7	$7\frac{1}{2}$	8	$9\frac{1}{2}$	11	12	$12\frac{1}{2}$	$13\frac{1}{2}$	14	16	17
BITCH 2	6	$5\frac{1}{2}$	5	5	5	5	5	6	6	6	Bitch	2 died

(Natural Birth)

DAY	13	14	15	16	17	18	19	20	21	4 Wks	5 Wks
DOG	15	15	$15\frac{1}{2}$	$15\frac{1}{2}$	$15\frac{1}{2}$	16	$16\frac{1}{2}$	18	19	31	40
BITCH 1	$17\frac{1}{2}$	18	19	20	21	22	23	24	24	35	42

(All weights in ounces)

By the time the two remaining puppies had reached eight weeks old there was no discrepancy in the weights.

Conditions of the bitch to be aware of during and after whelping are:

Inertia: This is a condition in which the usual powerful contractions of the uterus are either weak or absent. It can be divided into two types: *Primary Uterine Inertia* which can be caused by a variety of things. A bitch having had several litters could, because of her age and condition, suffer from inertia. Poor condition of the bitch may also cause inertia. A bitch who has suffered from primary inertia should not be used to breed from again. *Secondary Uterine Inertia* and which is very different from the first type. The bitch will normally start with contractions but for some reason these will become less. This may happen because a puppy has caused an obstruction and as a result the bitch will become tired and contractions will cease. Removal of the obstruction is necessary before serious damage occurs to the bitch. This will require the help of your vet and in many cases can result in a caesarean operation.

If you have puppies born to a bitch by caesarean operation and she has never delivered a puppy normally, either in previous litters or prior to the operation, take care when introducing the puppies back to her. Because the normal experiences of birth as stimuli are missing she may well resent the puppies and bitches have even been known to attack their puppies. Introduce them carefully and try to get the bitch to lick the puppies, this may help her to accept them. In any case you should not leave her alone until you are quite sure of her willingness to accept the normal maternal duties.

Eclampsia: This is a condition in the bitch caused by a lack of calcium in the blood. There are two danger periods after whelping and the first could occur at about ten days after whelping and the second when the puppies are about five weeks old. It is as well to know the symptoms as the condition should be treated as soon as it is noted as if left, the bitch will go into a coma. The first thing that may be noticed is stiffness in the legs. Other symptons include panting and uncontrolled shivering throughout the body and a staring expression. Eclampsia is treated by a vet giving an injection of calcium. Many vets recommend that the puppies of a bitch that has suffered from this condition should be hand reared to prevent any further strain on the bitch.

English and Irish Ch. Candida of Crinan.

11 Puppy Rearing

Birth to eight weeks

Apart from the attention of the bitch and the food she gives them, the most important requirement for a young puppy is warmth. This should be at a constant level but not so hot that the dam will continually leave her pups to cool down. The whelping box should also be free from draughts as at this stage in their lives puppies are unable to adjust to temperature changes.

If for some reason the dam is unable to feed her puppies it may be necessary to hand rear them or to find them a foster mother. I have heard of many people who have done this successfully, sometimes the foster mother being of the same breed and sometimes not. Great care must be taken to introduce the orphans. Remove the dam from her own puppies whilst introducing the newcomers. Try to put the scent of the bitch and the existing pups onto them before letting the bitch return, then watch her very carefully to make sure she settles down with them. Sometimes a bitch will produce milk if she has a phantom pregnancy and will rear an orphan litter.

In the event of no suitable bitch being available you will have to turn to hand rearing. Feeding the puppy should be kept as natural as possible. Foster feeding bottles and specially formulated milk are available for feeding orphan puppies and the manufacturer's instructions should be followed accurately. If you watch a puppy feeding from its mother you will notice that as it sucks it also pummels the bitch's tummy with its two front paws. When feeding a puppy you should allow it to suck and therefore an eye dropper is not altogether a good idea. It is more likely that the milk will go down the wrong way if a dropper or syringe is used. The best way to feed a puppy is to place a towel on your knee and place the puppy on the towel, facing away from you. Make the puppy reach a little for the teat on the bottle as in this way he will use his front paws in the same way as when feeding normally from the bitch. Another method that is successful is to let the puppy suck your little finger and at the same time slowly drip milk onto it, this again allows the same pummelling action to take place. Use can also be made of a warm water bottle wrapped up in a towel with the foster feeding bottle placed on top of this. For the first week it will be necessary to feed and clean the puppies every two hours, day and night. After the first week, if all is well and the puppies are putting on weight regularly, the feeds can be cut to three-hourly intervals and after about twelve days, the feed in the middle of the night can be dropped. At the same time the amount each puppy receives per feed should be increased. If

Bitch with her newly arrived litter of four puppies.

a puppy should fail to gain weight you must go back to the more regular feeding until weight gain is back to normal.

It is much easier to hand feed the litter if the mother is still available to attend to the puppies' bodily functions. A bitch does this by massaging their abdomens with her tongue. Should you be totally hand rearing a litter you will have to imitate this by using a piece of cotton wool to stimulate the puppies. This needs to be done after every feed.

At between three and five days the puppies' dew-claws can be removed by the vet. If only front dew-claws are present it is a matter for the individual to decide whether or not to have them taken off. Rear dew-claws occur very occasionally and hang very loose away from the leg on an adult dog and can quite easily be damaged and for this reason it is essential to have them removed at three to five days of age.

A healthy, normal puppy has an air of contentment. They rapidly lose the rather flat appearance of birth and become fat and round. They are quiet and not overactive, often they will be found lying on their backs with legs in the air. A litter that looks thin and who are noisy and continually moving around the box should give cause for concern. Check that they are warm enough and that the bitch has enough milk to feed them adequately.

Puppies' eyes open at between twelve and fifteen days but they do not focus until between twenty-one and twenty-eight days. Ears open after the eyes at about fourteen days.

During the period when the bitch is feeding the puppies, they will need a regular manicure as their nails become like little talons and if left unattended will start to scratch the bitch, so attend to this point regularly. I usually see to the nails once a week on the same day each week so that they are not forgotten.

One of the next things to attend to in the growing litter is worming. This used to be left until the litter was about five to six weeks old but this is now considered to be leaving it rather late. Puppies should be given their first worming dose at three weeks of age. Piperazene Citrate can be obtained from the vet and is excellent for small puppies. The dose must be repeated at intervals of fourteen days and this can be repeated until the puppies leave for their new homes at about eight weeks of age. Suggest to the new owner that the puppy can be wormed again when the final inoculation is given. The only worm that usually affects puppies in this country is *Toxacara Canis* and as this worm can be passed to humans, good hygiene should always be practised when dealing with young puppies in particular. Always wash your hands after cleaning up or handling the puppies and do not allow a young child to play with puppies before they have been thoroughly wormed. In any case children should be discouraged from

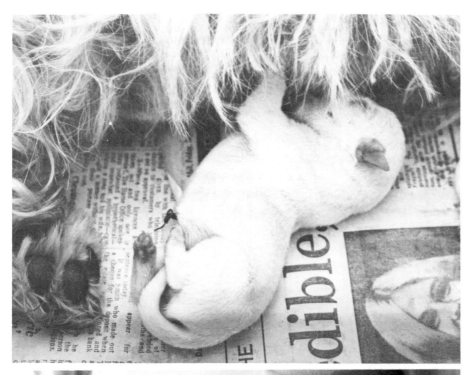

A one-day old pup feeding happily, note the umbilical cord, although dried out, has not yet fallen off.

A litter of 2-day-old pups. Still lacking pigment which will develop steadily over the next few days or weeks.

treating puppies as 'play things' and should be prevented from interfering with a litter whilst the mother is still nursing them.

It is difficult to give precise guidelines on weaning because each litter has to be treated differently. Some bitches love their puppies so much that it would be a cruel practice to take her away from them when they are only a few weeks old, other bitches are only too glad to see the back of them, just waiting for you to make the first move of giving them their first feed before thinking 'it's over to you'.

The methods of weaning are again as different as the time of weaning. I prefer to start weaning by using scraped meat or liquidised chicken in a little milk substitute. To begin with you may find that the puppies refuse a milky drink because they are still getting enough from the dam but you should still give them the opportunity to drink. You may need considerable patience when weaning puppies. Never leave them alone to feed. Continual supervision is needed to make sure each puppy gets a fair share and that they do not choke. Human baby foods can be used as an alternative, especially if the litter is small. To feed a large litter this way would be too expensive but is very convenient for only a couple of puppies.

Whichever method you use, weaning should be a gradual process and puppies should be allowed to continue to feed from their mother as well as from the owner. Do not try to introduce too many different foods at the same time as you will be likely to upset their tummies.

The bitch herself will probably aid weaning, sometimes when she is in with the puppies she will lie on her teats making them unavailable to the puppies or simply remove herself completely from their reach.

By the time the puppies are five weeks old they have their teeth and you will find that the bitch has become very reluctant to feed them. The pups will be more likely to take food from you and it will be necessary to feed at regular times. The main meals should be given in individual dishes but the milk feeds can still be fed communally, thus you will be able to check that each puppy has a fair share. After feeding they should have a nicely rounded tummy but not be bloated. At about six-and-a-half to seven weeks they should be independent of their mother for food when a typical diet could be:

Early morning: Warm milk with an added cereal or scrambled egg. Soft boiled egg can be given with a little cheese grated over it should a puppy become bored by the plain egg. Milk with baby cereal. Some puppies are unable to digest cow's milk and it would therefore be necessary to keep them on a substitute such as 'Lactol' or 'Whelpi'.

Mid-morning: A milky drink.

Mid-day: Small dish of minced or finely cut meat either raw or cooked, together with a small amount of well-soaked puppy meal. (Beef, chicken, rabbit or fish can be alternated.)

Tea: Repeat the mid-day feed, using one of the alternatives.

Bedtime: Warm milk with the addition of a cereal and honey or glucose. I usually give my puppies a wholemeal biscuit as a treat to chew at bedtime.

To one of the milk meals you should add Stress, Canovel or a similar preparation, according to the instructions on the container.

Eyes and ears now fully opened this puppy at just over 3 weeks old is becoming interested in his surroundings and is ready to explore.

This diet would be for an eight-week-old puppy and it should gradually change as the puppy gets older. As well as giving more for each feed you will find that the puppy will start to reject the milk meals in the morning and at bedtime and in this case the meat meals must be increased in quantity to make up for their loss. At the age of about seven months the mid-day meal can gradually be decreased until it is eliminated. At twelve months your West Highland should be on an adult diet which will vary according to its size but it should weigh about $\frac{1}{2}$lb (14g) of mixed meat and biscuit.

From about four weeks of age the puppies should be introduced to the household. House training should have already begun. After feeding the puppy should be encouraged to be clean in a place chosen by you. In the very early days this can be on newspaper in their play pen but by the time they reach four or five weeks, and if the weather is warm and still, they could be taken into the garden for a very short time to relieve themselves. It is amazing how quickly a very young puppy can be taught to be clean. A puppy allowed to run around in an uncleaned pen is very much harder to housetrain, so immediately a puppy soils a piece of paper remove it and replace it with a clean piece.

The puppies should, if possible, be allowed to mix with older dogs provided they have not been to dog shows or been mixing with other uninoculated dogs. This period is very important in a puppy's life as it is now that he learns to socialise. However, care must be taken because at this time the bitch's immunity is wearing off and the pups could become more likely to pick up disease. This has to be weighed against the fact that it is in these few weeks that the puppy learns to become a well balanced member of the family learning to take other dogs, children etc in its stride.

It is about this age that the puppy will be about ready to leave home. There are different thoughts about exactly when this should be. Some experts advocate that six weeks is the age at which they should go, as they adapt more quickly to their new home. Other breeders will not consider them going until they have had their second injections at fourteen weeks of age. The most common age at which the puppy starts his new life is eight weeks and this is the time that my puppies start life in their new homes.

When the puppies go to their new homes, it is kinder on the bitch if she has enjoyed her puppies and played with them, that you stagger their departure.

You have a responsibility to your puppies and if you feel any doubt about the suitability of a home, for whatever reason, have the guts to say 'NO' to the prospective purchaser.

When the purchasers come to collect their new charge, do point out any bad as well as good points the puppy may have and note these on a sales receipt so that no doubt is left about the quality of the puppy. Such things as being over or undershot or having an umbilical hernia should be clearly pointed out. If the client should seem at all reluctant do not try to change their minds, suggest that the puppy is taken to be vetted within twenty-four hours of leaving home. If the vet finds a defect that the new owner does not like – take the puppy back and return the purchase price. I find that if you have been totally honest about the puppy, this rarely happens. Never sell a very young puppy as a show dog because you never know how he may develop. All you can say is he is a fit, healthy puppy, possibly with show potential although it is better to sell puppies as companions and if they turn out to be a 'show stopper' so much the better.

The puppy should leave you with a clearly written pedigree, a sales receipt, Kennel Club registration certificate and a diet sheet. To this can be added a box of goodies with a supply of his usual diet to last a day or two and a favourite toy to help him settle into his new home.

Pedigree forms (for novices only)

The way in which pedigree forms are filled in may well fill the breed historian with horror. For the novice and onetime breeder, you must remember that the document is an important piece of paper which it is essential to fill in accurately and as neatly as possible. It is signed by you as being an accurate record of the breeding of a puppy. As the breeder of the puppies it is up to you to supply a pedigree for the purchaser. I have seen pedigrees with the most alarming mistakes and misspelt names.

Blank pedigree forms can be purchased in three, four or five generations and, more unusual, ten generations. The latter are usually in circular form and used by the owner of a dog as an interesting exercise because the work involved in their completion is vast. Five-generation forms are the best for a good quality pedigree dog as the purchaser can see at a glance the different lines which are in the breeding. It is usual when filling in the form to note the Champions in red and it is not at all unusual to have thirty-five or more Champions on the pedigree of a well-bred puppy. A blank form can look very daunting to someone who is unfamiliar with one. Look carefully at the form and you will notice a centre line which is an obvious division between the top half and bottom half of the form. The top part of the form is reserved for the father (sire) of the puppy and the lower is for the bitch's (dam) pedigree. Their names should appear in the first spaces on the left of the form.

You will have been given the pedigree of the sire of your puppies by the owner of the dog you used at stud. Normally this will be a printed card so you should take great care in copying it out as accurately as possible. If it is handwritten and there is a name that you are unable to read, do not guess what it should be but contact the owner and ask for clarification. Each name should be written in full, no part of it should be left out because of lack of space. When filling in your bitch's pedigree on the lower part of the form take equal care. Remember if there are any bitch puppies in the litter they may also be bred from and someone will need to read your writing when making out the forms for that litter. It is, therefore, a good idea to type the form or if that is not possible capital letters should be used.

As well as the names you can put on other useful information. Such things as Junior Warrants, important show wins or winners of certificates that are not champions are features of interest.

At the top of the form is a space for the name of the puppy as registered at the Kennel Club. There are also spaces provided for the name, address and phone number of yourself, the breeder, and on the other side, details of the puppy, its date of birth, sex, breed and Kennel Club registration number.

Kennel Club Registration

It is the responsibility of the breeder to provide Kennel Club Registration papers of some form to the purchaser of a puppy. A puppy that has not been registered by the breeder cannot have the omission rectified at a later date.

The first stage of registration is on a 'blue form' (form 1). This has to be completed by the breeder of the litter giving details of the bitch, the mating and the owner of the stud dog, confirming the mating. There are spaces for the date of mating as well as date of birth and number of puppies of each sex. You may be given the 'blue form' at the time of mating but many breeders prefer to hand them over after the birth of the litter. It does mean that the owner of the dam has to contact the stud dog owner and inform them of the outcome of the mating. In this way his stud receipt book can be kept up to date with the details of the mating.

A litter of puppies can be recorded only. In this case a purchaser will be given a form showing the details of the puppy and its sex but it will be unnamed. On purchasing the puppy the new owner will be able to name the puppy with their own choice of name but if you get this type of form you must not use the name of a dog that already appears on the pedigree as this name will be for the use of a certain breeder and no one else. These are known as an 'affix'.

If you are not given a form showing that your puppy is recorded at the Kennel Club you should be given the other alternative which is a puppy registration certificate. On this will be details of the puppy plus a name and number by which the Kennel Club will always be able to identify the puppy. If the puppy is shown or eventually bred from or used at stud, it is this name which must be used. On the reverse of the form is a section to be filled in by the person registered by the Kennel Club as the owner (in the case of a young puppy this will normally be the breeder). This section has to be filled in in order to transfer the puppy into your name. Next to this section is a similar one for you, the new owner, to complete. This should be done as soon as possible and sent with the relevant fee to the Kennel Club so that you can be registered as the new owner. Until this is done the previous owner will still be registered as the owner of the animal. This is most important, as if the dog is to be shown or bred from, this has to be done before he can appear with you as the owner. You could be disqualified if this is not done before show entries are sent off. If entries are to be

At eight weeks old these puppies are fully socialised and are ready to start life with their new owners.

placed before the forms are returned to you by the Kennel Club, they should be marked T.A.F. (Transfer applied for).

Other Kennel Club forms which may from time to time be necessary are:

Export Pedigree: For dogs which are to be exported from this country. The form is filled in with the pedigree of the dog and sent with the relevant fee to the Kennel Club. The Kennel Club check the pedigree of the dog and produce an authenticated pedigree. This is required by many overseas Kennel Clubs.

Junior Warrant Form: To be filled in by the owner of the show dog who has gained sufficient points (25) to claim a J.W. Certificate.

Breeder's Certificate: The breeder of a champion would be awarded this as opposed to the owner.

12 Ailments

In any breed of dog you can find a number of defects and medical problems, the West Highland being no exception. Some are known as inherited and others are believed to be so. Some develop in the foetus before birth and others appear later in the dog's life. In a breed as popular as the West Highland indiscriminate breeding for profit can multiply the results.

Many of the defects mentioned are thankfully fairly rare when one considers the overall number of the breed registered each year with the Kennel Club. Any new recruit to the breed should, however, have the knowledge of what may occur in a breeding programme.

C.M.O. (Craniomandibular osteopathy)

This is a fairly rare disease which is found in Cairns and Scottish Terriers as well as the West Highland White Terrier. It would appear to be inherited but it is not a simple pattern of inheritance. It is a disease which affects the lower jaw bone of the dog. Usually it is seen between four and seven months of age so it is important to differentiate by x-ray that it is C.M.O. and not a difficult teething.

The disease is an extraordinary growth in the cells of the bone where the mandible joins the skull. It usually affects both sides of the jaw. It is multiplication in growth of the bone cells and not bone cancer. There are signs that the disease goes through stages of growth and rest, so it may be thought to be cured by certain drugs before breaking out again. Another common name for C.M.O. is 'Lion Jaw'.

A puppy thought to have C.M.O. would exhibit signs of pain when trying to open his mouth and when eating but as mentioned before, similar signs can be seen in a puppy when teething. The only sure way of confirming the disease is an x-ray.

Various treatments are available from the vet. Cortisone is commonly used to control swelling but homeopathic remedies have been used with excellent results.

Dry eye (Keratoconjunctivitis sicca K.C.S.)

Much concern has been expressed by the veterinary fraternity about the incidence of 'dry eye' seen in the West Highland White Terrier. According to recent reports 'dry eye' is more prevalent in the West Highland than in any other breed and bitches are more frequently affected than dogs. More research is now being undertaken into this disease.

'Dry eye' occurs as a result of a decreased production of tears causing the eye to become inflamed. It affects the cornea which is the clear area in front of the eye and the conjunctiva which is the membrane surrounding the eye. Both eyes are usually affected but not necessarily at the same time or with equal severity.

The first sign of this disease is an excessive tackiness around the eyes. It is difficult to keep them clean and the discharge sticks to the margins of the eyelids. The eyes may become partly closed due to the lack of lubrication by tears and blinking may become painful. 'Dry eye' may also be linked with ear and skin problems in the same animals.

There are certain factors which are known to cause 'dry eye'. The use of certain drugs over a long period of time. Injury to the eye can also result in 'dry eye' but in this case it would only affect the damaged eye. In many 'Westies' the cause is not clear. In view of the large number of 'Westies' affected, it is suggested by the vets that there is a genetic factor involved although as yet no form of heredity has been proven.

Treatment takes two forms. The first is to lubricate the eyes several times a day with artificial tears, this treatment being continued throughout the rest of the dog's life.

The second treatment involves surgery. The salivary gland is diverted from the corner of the mouth to the corner of the eye, the saliva forming a lubricant for the eye. At first, after the operation, the eye will often 'water' excessively and need to be cleaned frequently but the flow of saliva gradually slows down.

At the present time the Unit of Comparative Ophthalmology at the Animal Health Trust is carrying out further research into the condition.

Perthes disease (Pseudo Leg Perthes, Legg-Calve)

This is probably the most alarming complaint from which a West Highland can suffer. It also affects other short-legged terriers indigenous to Scotland, as well as humans.

No evidence has been found to show that the condition is hereditary. In fact, the most favoured theory for its occurrence in dogs is that it is caused by an injury such as a game of football when the ball has struck the dog on the hip. Another theory is that it is caused by a nutritional fault. As yet,

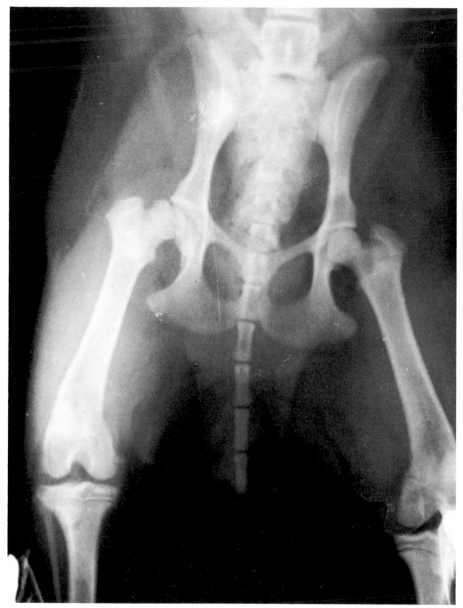

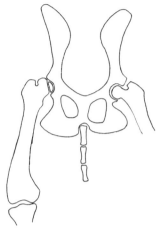

FIG 30 Diagram clarifying x-ray of the hips of a dog suffering from Perthes: the growing head is separated from the rest of the femur.

An x-ray of the hips of a West Highland suffering from Perthes. This became apparent in this bitch at eight months of age just before she came into season. The diagram above clarifies the x-ray.

not enough research has been done on the condition as seen in dogs to come to any positive conclusions.

The disease is usually seen between the ages of four and ten months and is extremely painful. The dog will limp on his hind legs, it can be one or both legs that are affected, and as the disease progresses, the muscles of the leg become wasted.

Perthes is caused by the cutting off of the blood supply to the head of the femur. In the developing dog and child, the head of the femur is not firmly fixed in place but has a blood supply between the main bone and the extreme head where it fits into the pelvis. In the adult these become fused together and perthes can no longer occur. If the blood supply becomes disconnected from the head, the head itself dies and becomes disconnected from the rest of the femur, causing wearing of the bone within the hip joint. Consequently the dog feels pain and limps to relieve that pain.

Two forms of treatment are available, one is to keep the dog on drugs to reduce the inflammation, until eventually the bone recalcifies. The other form of treatment is to remove the small piece of bone (about the size of a little finger nail). At first the dog will walk on the three remaining sound legs but eventually the muscles will strengthen and the dog will be able to walk normally.

Although this is a very upsetting thing for both dog and owner to go through, it will make no difference to the life of the dog as a companion. All breeders do their best to avoid breeding a bad litter or one with obvious faults and this is one disease which seems impossible to avoid as it can appear suddenly without any previous history having been noted. Usually only one puppy in a litter is affected. Perhaps with more research answers will be found as to why it occurs.

Dermatitis

Perhaps the greatest cause for visits to the vet by the 'Westie' owner is skin trouble. About nine out of ten visits will be for this problem. Some 'Westies' are prone to this whilst others are completely clear all their lives.

Allergies in the human population are only just starting to be investigated by the medical profession and dogs are rather behind them. Allergies to food additives and modern materials are now commonplace. The same allergies will also be likely to affect the canine population.

The best friend that a dog with skin trouble can have is a very observant owner. So often the dog will have been scratching or nibbling for some time before an owner will do anything about the problem. When grooming a dog it is easy to see if a dog is becoming itchy because if you run your hand over the coat it will promote a twitching response. Dogs that are clipped are not encouraged to have a healthy skin and coat as dead hair blocks the hair follicles. Stripping or the removal of dead hair will allow the coat to grow more healthily. Also if the coat is clipped very short in summer, with the mistaken idea that the dog is being kept cooler, damage and irritation can be caused by the sun and various pollens. Frequent baths can also dry the skin by removing the natural oils and this should be avoided. The more frequently you wash your West Highland, the quicker he will get dirty.

Eczema

Apart from parasitic infestation, this is the other main cause for itching in the West Highland. All skin problems arising from internal disturbances can be classed under this heading. The causes of eczema are many and can be unsuitable diet or side effects of drugs or it may be a sensitive skin which reacts abnormally to hand stripping or clipping or a bite of any type.

Whatever the cause the results have to be treated in two ways. The first is to stop the local cause of irritation and the second is to find the source of the trouble and remove it.

Eczema may appear in many forms it can be a red patch on the skin which is further inflamed by constant chewing and scratching. It may be dry and scaley or there may even be patches of skin which continually break and are wet.

Probably the best thing to do in the first place is to change the diet. It may be that the food you are feeding is too rich for the dog; on the other hand the diet may be deficient in some important constituent. If the dog is fed on an all-in-one food where meat does not need to be added because it is there in dry form, try changing to a wholemeal biscuit mixed with white meat or fish. If you have been adding red meat this could well mean that it was far too rich. Yeast tablets could be fed at the same time. A different diet worth trying is the regime suggested by Buster Lloyd-Jones and made by Denes. The tinned meat in this range uses white meat and includes carrots and comfrey which is a herb used to aid internal healing.

The changes of diet that you can make are as varied as the types of eczema and each change you make must be given a reasonable time to have an effect.

At the same time as a change of diet you must deal with the external evidence. Something soothing is what is needed and a vet may be able to suggest some form of external medication. A dilute form of T.C.P. may be used on wet areas, dabbing it gently onto the affected area. Preparations are available from the pet shop which bare some resemblance to calamine lotion and this can be very soothing. Cream made specially for use on skin troubles can also be tried.

If all these experiments bring no improvement and you have not found any obvious cause, a vet must be consulted, in fact the previous experiments may even have been suggested by your vet as a preliminary. Eczema can be treated with steroids but the side effects can be as distressing as the condition itself and should be embarked upon with caution. Cultures can be made from the skin condition itself and used in injection form to treat the dog. In the only case that I have seen treated like this, the results were dramatic. After being treated on cortisone for several years the dog began a course of treatment at a University Veterinary Department and soon the side effects of the original course of treatment had disappeared, his skin returned to its normal colour and his coat grew properly again. He is now a happy little dog again and only very occasionally does his skin cause trouble, this being only slight it can easily be dealt with externally by his owners.

So having found the cause or dealt with the condition it is extremely important to keep a careful eye on the skin and avoid any recurrence of the initial outbreak.

Contact allergy

This can usually be traced to something around the house, perhaps the allergy only starts after a new piece of furniture or carpet has arrived in the home. Sometimes the allergy can be to man-made fibres; in other cases it can be the filling in pillows or furniture. It can sometimes be rather puzzling to the vet unused to a West Highland's idiosyncrasies. The allergy may appear down the back of the dog and a vet might not realise that a 'Westie's' favourite sleeping position is on his back with his legs in the air. A vet would quite reasonably expect a contact allergy to be on the dog's legs or tummy. The only way to treat this form of allergy is to remove the source of irritation or to keep the dog away from it.

In summer 'Westies' are sometimes prey to skin allergies brought on by various types of pollen. Grasses quite frequently cause an allergic response which dies down as the pollens decrease in autumn.

Fleas

The most common cause of itchiness is fleas or allergy to flea saliva, so every effort should be made to keep the dog free from fleas. Once bitten by a flea the dog will scratch or chew the itchy spots thus making them worse, so the initial condition must never be ignored.

FIG 31 Parasites (not drawn to scale)

The first sign that your dog has fleas will probably be seen when he is being groomed. Small black sand-like grains will be seen in areas along the back, particularly in front of the tail and around the shoulder blades. The fleas themselves, although they move very fast, are easy to see on a white dog and it is easy to catch them and kill them between the finger nails. However, the fleas have probably laid eggs and the dog should be bathed at regular intervals in insecticidal shampoo to make sure that any new eggs hatching out are dealt with.

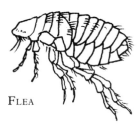

FLEA

Besides fleas there are other forms of livestock that can cause itching and distress to the dog.

Harvest mites

These are small red parasites which look like grains of sand. They can be seen around the feet and under the armpits. They appear at harvest time and are more troublesome in some areas of the country than in others.

MITE

Lice

These are minute blood-suckers and can easily be overlooked unless a close examination is made. They are very light coloured and have the look of dandruff. Only when they are magnified will they be seen to move. In the beginning they will gather around the neck and ears and along the back but will later spread over the whole dog.

Rabbit mites

These also have the appearance of scurf unless inspected microscopically. They are more likely to be seen on puppies.

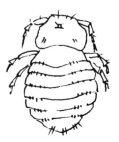

BITING LOUSE

The best treatment for these infestations is regular baths in a good insecticidal shampoo supplied by the vet. It would be necessary to repeat the baths at regular intervals to kill off any eggs which may hatch out after the first batch have been killed. You may have to repeat the process several times to be totally successful. As well as treating the dog, all bedding must be thoroughly cleaned and disinfected every time the dog is bathed.

Ticks

These are most likely to be found in sheep country, being left on grass and bushes that have been passed by sheep. They are blood-suckers that attach themselves by their jaws into the skin of the dog. The easiest way to remove them is to dab them with methylated spirits, thus making them release their grasp, they can then be removed individually. It is essential to remove the head as well as the body and if they are merely pulled off this would not happen and the skin would become sore and infected. A dog taken for walks regularly in sheep country should be thoroughly checked daily, as if left, the ticks could become a health hazard.

SUCKING LOUSE

Mange

There are two types of mange:
Sarcoptic: This is very contagious and will spread from one dog to another. It will follow a set pattern in its development. The irritation

ENLARGED FEMALE TICK

usually starts around the feet spreading to the ears and around the eyes where bare patches will develop. The trouble will then spread up the legs and under the chest and stomach, round the tail and under the nose and chin. Although this pattern makes diagnosis fairly easy, it is necessary to have an examination of a skin scraping to confirm the condition.

Treatment has to be thorough and must be repeated several times but it will respond and can be cleared up.

Follicular: Fortunately this complaint is fairly rare. Its treatment and cure are very difficult.

It is caused by a small creature which burrows deeply into the follicles of the skin. It is from this that the name is taken. For the simple reason that the cause is so deeply buried it becomes difficult to treat.

The symptoms are that the skin becomes thickened, wrinkled and greyish in appearance. The feet are usually attacked first, from where it spreads up the legs to the stomach and around the head and ears. Although the undercoat falls out the top coat remains although it looks rather sparse and there is a strange mousey smell connected with the condition. It is not very contagious and seems to like certain types of skin.

Bitches with follicular mange should not be bred from as the complaint will be passed on to her offspring, in what way it is not certain but because of the difficulty of a permanent cure it would be unfair to expect any puppy to suffer for the whole of its life.

Ringworm

This is uncommon and is caused by a fungus. It is easily diagnosed as small rings which are bald and crusty. It is very contagious and immediate treatment should be carried out and all other dogs carefully watched. Ringworm can also spread to humans so special precautions should be taken. Veterinary supervision is necessary and instructions should be very carefully complied with.

Inguinal hernia

The inguinal canals are on each side of the stomach and failure for this canal to close properly may allow a loop of the intestines to protrude into the canal. At birth this type of hernia is difficult to detect but usually becomes visible when the puppy starts to take solid foods. The enlargement should be replaced as much as possible. Eventually the puppy will need an operation to correct the hernia. A vet will usually operate as soon as the puppy has finished his course of preventative injections. It should, however, be dealt with as soon as possible because of the possibility of further complications.

Cleft palate
This is a condition found in many breeds. It is seen in new-born puppies. The boney roof of the mouth which separates the mouth from the nasal passages fails to close. A puppy will quickly die of starvation or pneumonia because any milk which the puppy manages to get will take the wrong route. This could be down the nose or into the lungs. Puppies should be checked at birth and if a cleft palate is found the kindest thing for bitch and puppy is to put it down. This puppy, if left with the bitch, would be liable to distress her and it would be extremely callous to cause it unnecessary suffering.

TAPEWORM

Slipping patella
The patella is the knee cap of the dog and in some dogs causes problems by moving from the correct position, causing the dog to limp.

ROUNDWORM

Pancreatitis
The pancreas fails to function properly or not at all and the dog loses weight. The condition can be treated by capsules made from the pig's pancreas.

Ear troubles
It is unusual for a West Highland to get trouble in the ears because, with their prick ears, there is a good and free flow of air.

Once a dog has had a problem, be it with wax or ear mites, there does seem to be a tendency for it to return, so thorough and prompt attention should be given and it is wise to do this under the direction of your vet. To poke into a dog's ear without knowledge could cause permanent damage.

Ear troubles can be parasitical or non-parasitical. The ear mite of the cat, which is quite common, is quite happy to inhabit a dog's ear so if there are cats in the house or if cats regularly cross the area frequented by your dog, you should make regular checks. The presence of a moist brown deposit could indicate their presence, but they would have to be checked by your vet. Other irritants could be grass seeds, particularly at harvest time and possibly sand if you have spent your holiday at the seaside.

If the inside of the ear is permanently damaged by disease or continual infection, the membranes inside the ear thicken and if nothing is done the dog will become deaf and will be in constant pain. The treatment is an operation to cut the canal to widen the opening into the ear and allow more space between the membranes. It is not always effective and does affect the ear carriage (it usually drops) so this would detract from his appearance and make him unacceptable in the show ring.

Alternative treatments for dogs
As alternative treatments become available for humans, the same methods
are also made available for the canine population. In this age of widespread
use of drugs, many people who have the welfare of animals at heart are
concerned to cut down the use of man-made drugs and are looking at older
therapies. All drugs have their place in the treatment of animal health but
there is now a widespread belief that if drugs are kept until they are really
necessary they will be more effective.

There are numerous forms of therapy but three which are used quite
frequently are acupuncture, herbs and homoeopathy.

Acupuncture: This is available for dogs but if the acupuncturist is not a vet
your vet's permission must be given before the dog can be treated.
Greyhound owners make use of this form of therapy to treat damaged
muscles caused by racing. I have also made use of acupuncture on a dog
who lost the use of his hind legs.

Herbal therapies: These are widely used by many people, sometimes
without really realizing that they are using them. Herbal remedies are
readily available on various trade stands at dog shows and are widely used
by many exhibitors. Probably the best known would be raspberry leaf
tablets given to bitches in whelp or kelp to aid pigment. Greenleaf can be
given to help cleanse the blood and to neutralise excess acid and can also be
used in cases of rheumatism, eczema and kidney conditions. There are
many others which can be tried for specific problems.

Homoeopathy: This is perhaps the least understood of all the alternative
therapies. The name is derived from the Greek word '*Homoios*' meaning
'like'. Homoeopathy is the practice of treating like with like, that is to say,
treating the illness with a substance that produces the same symptoms as
those displayed by the patient. Homoeopathy, unlike modern medicine,
sees the symptoms as the body's reaction against the illness and its
attempts to overcome it and tries to stimulate the reaction not suppress it.

Its success depends on the owner knowing his dog extremely well, his
temperament and habits and preferences. All information is important
when deciding on necessary treatment.

Many vets are becoming interested in using homoeopathy as well as
conventional forms of treatment. Some breeders swear by it and use it for
all forms of treatment including the prevention of all the usual puppy
diseases.

As I mentioned herbs for various conditions, so those same conditions can be treated as follows:

Whelping   Caulophyllum
Eczema   Psorinum, Sulphur, Arsen Alb, Petroleum, Merc. Corr.
            Graphites (each type of eczema needing a different remedy).

Several interesting books are now available on the subject.

Before embarking on any form of treatment it is as well to discuss your ideas with your own vet and make sure of his approval.

13 Looking after the older Dog

As your dog passes from maturity to old age, the passing of time will show its effects. Stiffening joints make chasing next door's cat just that bit more difficult and the cheeky sparrow is now able to approach the bird table without constant shouts of warning that he is not the owner of the garden.

Things must be taken into account to make an older 'Westie's' life a little more easy. On the whole West Highlands live to a ripe old age with a great deal of bounce more than many half their age in another breed.

An old dog's digestion may not be quite so good as in the past and it is a good idea to split up their daily meal into two, so as not to put too much of a strain on them.

Care must be taken of his general health, check his teeth regularly as a bad tooth would affect the gums and cause gingivitis, this can also cause other more serious illnesses. Skin, nails, feet and ears should be regularly inspected and problems dealt with. It is just as important to keep the old dog well groomed and his coat in good condition. Many older dogs find standing to be stripped very hard and it may be necessary to deal with the coat in stages. It may even be necessary to resort to clipping or cutting the coat. Some dogs get a more tender skin with ageing and stripping can cause tenderness. Any injuries to the spine may also mean that stripping is uncomfortable for them. Always do what makes life easier for the oldie.

Sometimes the owner will not realise when something is amiss with the dog. If his tummy becomes distended and he has had nothing extra to eat, the vet should be consulted as this could be a sign of more serious problems. An old dog sitting and panting excessively is unlikely to be hot, it is more likely to be a sign of heart trouble. This recently happened to my own fifteen year old, he even found taking a few steps an effort. It was unfortunate that nothing could be done to help him so I took the only step possible. He had had a long and happy life and it would have been cruel to prolong it.

Any deviation from what is normal for your dog should be dealt with without delay, as it may cause extra stress to the old dog. Drinking a great

An old dog approaching fifteen years of age still enjoying life pottering around the garden and going for short walks.

deal more water than usual may be an outward sign of kidney or liver trouble or stones, prostate or womb trouble and should be checked without delay.

An older dog may tend to feel the cold more than in his younger days so make sure that his bed is placed in a warm, draught-free position. If he goes out for a walk and returns wet, make sure that he is dried off thoroughly.

If life eventually is obviously getting too much of a burden for him and he no longer has any enjoyment in the small pleasures of life, you have to come to the final decision to release him from his burden. It would be wrong to let him suffer when he has given so much for so long. If this has to happen to your dog, do not desert him at the end but stay with him and at least he will be with someone he knows at the end.

14 Beyond the Show Ring

Not everyone is interested in showing their West Highland but there are other pursuits where you can have much pleasure with your dog. In this country obedience competition is very strong but abroad many other pursuits are available to the Highlander and owner. Tracking and working trails are held for terriers where they can be taught to follow a scent laid down for them, also false tunnels are laid for a terrier to go to ground.

The 'Westie' is a compact and very intelligent little dog, full of bounce and energy, he is well suited to these other pursuits. Unfortunately very little of this type of competition happens in this country and we have to look at the scene abroad to give more details about the fun we are missing in this country.

Obedience

Although it is very easy to join an obedience class in this country the majority of dogs used are German Shepherds and Border Collies, other breeds are usually in the minority. Only very few West Highlands have ventured into the obedience ring with any success.

To join an obedience class it may be necessary to enrol on a course of lessons. It is a good idea to start basic training at as early an age as possible. At about four months of age the dog is receptive to learning what you want him to do.

Simple obedience is important and every puppy should be taught to walk to heel on a slack lead. This will do no harm even for a dog who is to be shown; however, it is not wise for the show dog to do more advanced obedience training as there is nothing more infuriating than having a dog sit immediately you stop, when all you wanted him to do was to stand for the judge to inspect him.

A 'Westie' should be well known for his ability to learn and willingness to please. He is very intelligent and will find learning exercises quite within his scope but will become very bored by continuous repetition. 'Westies' like to please but it must also be fun, so once you sense that he is becoming bored, stop the exercise. Perhaps one of the more difficult things for a 'Westie' to learn is a straight sit. Normally he will sit with a rather lop-sided attitude with one back leg sticking out sideways.

'Westman' working. Int. and Nordic Ch. Busheys Magic Storm was Swedish 'Dog of the Year' in 1982. In 1984 he was awarded the Swedish Sportsman's Association, Prize of Honour for his skill as a tracker dog.

Tracking

'Westies' should find much excitement and interest in pursuing this part of the sport, unfortunately it is not something that takes place in Britain. Both the U.S.A. and Sweden hold tests for tracking which in America leads to the title of T.D. (Tracker Dog). This can be seen after the name of any dog who has qualified.

Tracking is carried out in an open field, the dog wearing a harness with a lead some 20 to 40 feet (6 to 12m) long attached. The dog has to follow a scent which is laid before the test takes place. There may be right-angled turns so that the dog has to follow the scent up and down wind.

'Westies' in the public eye

The Westie in Advertising: Dogs are always used by advertisers in one way or another. It is becoming interesting to spot the West Highland as new adverts appear. The most famous brand to use a West Highland must surely be 'Black and White' whisky. For many years the West Highlands of the Gaywyn Kennels were used for the photographic sessions, Ch. Alpingay Sonata being the star for many years.

Perhaps the most sought after calendar of the year is that produced for

Pirelli – usually full of glamorous young ladies. On one occasion the glamorous 'granny' Ch. Fanny MacDougal appeared on its glossy pages, she even appeared in the Sunday colour supplement of a well-known newspaper!

Highlanders as personalities: Do you remember seeing the article in the newspapers a few years ago about the 'Westie' who had received a summons to appear for jury service? I think the judge would have received a surprise had he arrived to take his place.

Recently two West Highland White Terriers were the guests of honour at the reopening of the West Highland line by British Rail. The proud guests were Incheril Evita and Incheril Rowena owned by Mrs Ela Berry. See if you can spot the locomotive which carries the symbol of a West Highland on the side of the engine.

Elaine Page, the singer, is the owner of a West Highland 'Tugger' made famous in his own right by his antics when he appeared on T.V. He took exception to a toy terrier brought on by Freddie Starr the comedian and gave a show of his terrier temperament.

The 'Westie' in art

Being such a strong personality the West Highland has always been an important model for the artist. With his dark eyes and rather cheeky expression, he has always been able to catch the eye of the public; artists are no exception to this.

Although the breed has not been around for very long, artists with a canine interest have always chosen him to paint. Some of the very early prints produced in the second half of the nineteenth century show dogs that bear some resemblance to the West Highland but could easily be put down as Skye Terriers or even Cairns. Probably the most famous of the early paintings of the breed which is unmistakable is the painting 'Dignity and Impudence' by the artist Sir Edwin Landseer R.A. This painting has been reproduced in many forms and may be found on many objects produced during the late nineteenth century and early twentieth century. Tin objects can still quite often be found bearing this very famous image. Money boxes and boxes used to pack biscuits are very collectable and can still be found at a reasonable price on antique stands at dog shows. The firm of Jenner and Bettridge were highly regarded for their work in papier-mâché in the late nineteenth century and they too used the famous images of the hound and West Highland as painted by Landseer.

Artists on both sides of the Atlantic have been fascinated by the breed

Over the years Buchanan's have produced objects for 'Black & White' Whisky which are considered collectable.

A group of objects depicting 'Dignity and Impudence'.

and their work forms an interesting record of the early development of the West Highland.

During the early part of the twentieth century the canine artist Arthur Wardle was actively engaged in painting all breeds of dog but he seemed to be very strongly drawn to the terriers. He has produced many beautiful paintings of the West Highland. He captures in his paintings, the intelligence and charm which obviously drew him to paint the breed. The quality of his paintings is such that they are now considered works of art, not just mementos of the breed. They are in great demand and whenever one appears at auction, large prices are paid, such is the appeal of his work. As well as paintings, Wardle produced pen and ink and pencil drawings of the breed. So although to most of us the paintings of Arthur Wardle are unobtainable, it is still possible to have a modest representation of his work in the form of contemporary cards.

Another artist to be drawn to the breed and to have painted him regularly is Maud Earl. The breed itself has, in its history, had followers who are themselves artists. On both sides of the Atlantic and in Scandinavia there are people who are active in the breed and are also gifted artists in both two and three dimensions.

In America one such artist was Miss Dorothy Hardcastle who had an enormous talent for capturing the essence of the breed in oils. It is not only in paint that the 'Westie' is captured. The artists Dee Burdick, David Ogg and Tom Drexler are renowned in their own country for the quality of their work in clay. They have between them produced many beautiful models of the West Highland, both as a show dog and in more playful moments.

In addition to work done by our own breeders, many of the famous makers of porcelain have turned to the West Highland for inspiration, amongst them are Beswick, Royal Doulton and Royal Copenhagen. There are also many less well known manufacturers producing 'Westie' models, Northern Light and Heredities being only two that come to mind.

Some models of West Highlands.

I myself gain much inspiration from my own dogs for oil paintings and models. It is not only the face that can inspire the artist. My most lasting impression of two of my dogs is of them disappearing down a hole, leaving only their back ends visible, but being told by their tails exactly what it was that they thought they could smell down there.

Besides works of art there are many collectables picturing the West Highland and it can become a very time consuming hobby which can give you much pleasure.

And finally

To new breeders, the future of this delightful breed is in your hands. It has been nurtured carefully through generations by many knowledgeable people dedicated to the breed. It is for you to protect and guard against the whims of fashion and to keep the true character and style of the West Highland which makes it 'just that' and not merely another terrier. Never miss any opportunity to learn from the older, more experienced breeder. You will never know it all – if you think you do – THINK AGAIN!

Appendix 1

Winners of the Macconachie Trophy – 1951 to 1985

(Awarded annually by the West Highland White Terrier Club of England for the West Highland gaining most Challenge Certificates in that year.)

1951	Ch. Staplands Shepherd	Mr & Mrs Walsh	Dog
1952	Ch. Wolvey Piquet	Mrs C.J. Pacey	Bitch
1953	Ch. Calluna the Poacher	Mrs A. Beels	Dog
1954	Ch. Tulyar of Trenean	Mrs W. Dodgson	Dog
1955	Ch. Rowmore Brora of Kennishead	Miss I.R. Maclean Cowie	Dog
1956	Ch. Wolvey Pied Piper	Mrs C.J. Pacey	Dog
1957	Ch. Banker of Branston	Mrs D.M. Dennis	Dog
1958 {	Ch. Brindie of Branston	Mrs D.M. Dennis	Bitch
	Ch. Rivelin Rustle	Mrs M.W. Pearson	Bitch
1959	Ch. Bavena of Branston	Mrs D.M. Dennis	Bitch
1960	Ch. Bandsman of Branston	Mrs D.M. Dennis	Dog
1961	Ch. Brenda of Branston	Mrs D.M. Dennis	Bitch
1962	Ch. Alpin of Kendrum	The Hon. T.H. Rollo	Dog
1963	Ch. Busybody of Branston	Mrs D.M. Dennis	Bitch
1964	Ch. Quakertown Quistador	Mrs K. Sansom	Dog
1965	Ch. Quakertown Quistador	Mrs K. Sansom	Dog
1966	Ch. Pillerton Peterman	Mrs S.J. Kearsey	Dog
1967 {	Ch. Alpinegay Impresario	Mrs B.M. Wheeler	Dog
	Ch. Morenish Geordie	Mrs G. Wallace	Dog
1968	Ch. Rhianfa Up and Coming of Estcoss	Mrs V.L. Estcourt	Bitch
1969	Ch. Lorell Last Legacy	Mrs M. Duell	Dog
1970	Ch. Cedarfell Messenger Dove	Mr H. Painting	Bitch
1971	Ch. Checkbar Tommy Quite Right	Mrs J. Taylor	Dog
1972	Ch. Cedarfell Merry-N-Bright	Mrs M.P. Coy	Dog

1973	Ch. Sarmac Heathstream Drummer Boy	Mrs E.A.A. Millen	Dog
	Ch. Ardenrun Andsome of Purston	Mr M. Collings	Dog
1974	Ch. Dianthus Buttons	Mrs K. Newstead	Dog
1975	Ch. Glengordon Hannah	Mrs M. Torbet	Bitch
1976	Ch. Glenalwyne Sonny Boy	Miss J. Herbert	Dog
1977	Ch. Glenalwyne Sonny Boy	Miss J. Herbert	Dog
1978	Ch. Domaroy Saracen	Mr & Mrs R. Wilshaw	Dog
1979	Ch. Olac Moondrift	Mr D. Tattersall	Dog
1980	Ch. Furzeleigh Startrec	Mr J. Hodsall	Dog
1981	Ch. Halfmoon of Olac	Mr D. Tattersall	Bitch
1982	Ch. Haweswalton Houdini	Mrs S. Hawes	Dog
1983	Ch. Haweswalton Sportsman	Mrs S. Hawes	Dog
1984	Ch. Midshipman of Haweswalton	Mrs S. Hawes	Dog
1985	Ch. Clan Crinan	Mrs B. Hands	Dog

Appendix 2

Some British affixes and their owners of today

Angilgate	Mrs B. Strivens	Kilbrannon	Mr & Mrs R. Webster
Arnholme	Mrs D. Parr	Kristajen	Mrs J. Abbey
Aronstan	Miss M. Stone	Lasara	Mrs B. Graham and Miss J. Kabel
Ashgate	Mr & Mrs A. Thomson	Leastar	Mr & Mrs B. Lester
Backmuir	Mrs I. Gellan	Lochclae	Mr & Mrs R. Clay
Ballacoar	Mrs S. Morgan	Lorell	Mrs M. Duell
Birkfell	Miss S. Cleland	Lusundy	Mrs H. Dangerfield
Calluna	Miss A.A. Wright	Melwyn	Mrs R. Pritchard
Carillyon	Mrs T. Lees	Morenish	Miss E.C. Grieve
Cedarfell	Mrs M. Coy	Newtonglen	Mrs M. Torbet
Clanestar	Mrs D.K. Lancaster	Olac	Mr & Mrs D. Tattersall
Cranella	Mr & Mrs S. Bunting	Olton	Mr R.C. Hill and Mr M.P. Wilson
Crinan	Mrs B. Hands	Pillerton	Mrs S. Kearsey
Crookfields	Mr & Mrs F. Shereston	Poolmist	Mr & Mrs R. Foulkes
Danelea	Mr & Mrs K. Gourlay	Quakertown	Mrs H. Sansom
Domaroy	Mr & Mrs R. Wilshaw	Rivelin	Mrs W. Pearson
Famecheck	Miss F.M.C. Cook	Roneval	Miss E. Macallan
Furzeleigh	Mr & Mrs J. Hodsall	Rotella	Mr R. Wright
Gaelic Glory	Mrs D.I. Martin	Sarmac	Mrs A. Millen
Gaywyn	Miss C. Owen	Snojo	Mr & Mrs T.W. Johnson
Gilbri	Mr & Mrs B. Broom and Family	Suebeck	Mr & Mrs P. Mitchell
Glenalwyne	Miss J. Herbert	Sumar	Miss S. Jackson
Greenshire	Mr & Mrs J. Hammond	Sumway	Mr & Mrs J. Shelley
Guilliland	Mr J. Guthrie	Tasman	Mr & Mrs A. Bonas
Haweswalton	Mr & Mrs K. Hawes	Trethmore	Miss E.M. Wilson
Highstile	Mr & Mrs T. Bertram	Valucis	Mrs J. Williams
Incheril	Mr & Mrs E.M. Berry	Wistmill	Miss J. Johnson
Justrite	Mr & Mrs R. Armstrong	Woodpuddle	Mrs C. Ingram

Appendix 3

Useful addresses

The Kennel Club,
1 Clarges Street,
London W1.

The West Highland White Terrier Club
Mrs I. Gellan,
Mayfield Kennels,
Carnock Road,
Dunfermline,
Fife,
Scotland.

The West Highland White Terrier Club (of England)
Mrs J. Abbey,
7 Pottery Lane,
Woodlesford,
Leeds,
Yorks.

The North of Ireland West Highland White Terrier Club
Mrs M. Johnston,
24 Corkhill Road,
Seskinore,
Co. Tyrone.

The Southern West Highland White Terrier Club
Mrs M. Dickinson,
42 Southview Drive,
Upminster,
Essex. RM14 2LD.

There is a breed rescue scheme in operation and initially you should contact Mrs B. Graham for help or enquiries. Her address is:

Mrs B. Graham,
Lasara Kennels,
Kiln Farm,
Oxford Road,
Stokenchurch,
Bucks. HP14 3YH.

There are also representatives in other parts of the country.

The 'Westie' Rescue Scheme is a Registered Charity.

Appendix 4

Bibliography

The West Highland White Terrier
by Barbara Hands   Bartholomew

Westie!
by Birgitta Hasselgren   Nya

The Complete West Highland White Terrier
by John T. Marvin   Howell Books

The West Highland White Terrier
by Mary M. Dennis and C. Owen   Popular Dogs

A Photographic Record since 1899
by G.B. Dennis

Westies from Head to Tail
by Ruth Faherty   Alpine Pub. Inc.

The Kennelgarth Scottish Terrier Book
by Betty Penn-Bull   Saiga Pub. Co. Ltd

Practical Dog Breeding and Genetics
by Eleanor Frankling   Popular Dogs

Reproductive Clinical Problems in the Dog
by D.E. Jones and J.O. Joshua   Wright P.S.G.

The Treatment of Dogs by Homoeopathy
by K. Sheppard   Health Science Press

Homoeopathy for Pets
by George MacLeod   Homoeopathic Development
Foundation Ltd

Complete West Highland White Terrier
edited by J & L Cartledge   Ebury Press

West Highland White Terriers
by May Pacey   Foyles

Know your West Highland White Terrier
by Earl Schneider   The Pet Library Ltd

West Highland White Terrier
by Holland Buckley   Illustrated Kennel News Co. Ltd

Index

Page numbers in *italic* refer to illustrations